Alex Williams

•

Holy Spy

for Frank & Susan
and your wonderful family
May God bless, keep &
use you — always
Alex Williams

Phil 4[4]

HOLY SPY

Stories from Eastern Europe
by
Alex Williams

Copyright: © Alex Williams 2003

ISBN: 963 9148 92 X (HARMAT)
ISBN: 1 85792 906 3 (CFP)

Cover design: © Istvan Lente, Debrecen, Hungary

Published in 2003 jointly by Harmat Publishing,
Bukarest utca 3, H-1114 Budapest, Hungary, www.harmat.hu
and by Christian Focus Publication Ltd,
Geanies House, Fearn, TAIN, IV201TW, Scotland, www.christianfocus.com

Visit: www.holyspy.com

All rights reserved. No part of this publication may be reproduced, stored in a retrieval system, or trasnmitted, in any form or by any means, electronic, mechanical, photocopying, recording or otherwise, without prior premission of one of the publishers.

Printed and bound in Hungary

Contents

Foreword by Sir Fred Catherwood ...*6*
Dedication and Acknowledgements ...*8*
Introduction ...*10*
Wedding in Hungary ...*14*
Maps ...*19*
Days of Small Things ...*20*
Inside the Weird World of Eastern Europe ...*26*
Crumbling Communism ...*34*
Laying the Foundations ...*49*
Guests and Graduates. ...*59*
Chasing Christians, Chasing Birds ...*90*
Polish Prelude ...*106*
Polish Progress ...*123*
Bare Foot Doctor at Work ...*132*
Camps and Conferences—People and Places ...*138*
A Visit to Students in the Soviet Union ...*141*
Life in Romania ...*142*
Africans in Bucharest ...*148*
Beginning of Books and End of an Era for Arne ...*153*
Broken Leg and Unblocked Toilet in Poland ...*155*
The Vision for Bielice ...*159*
Wardens for Bielice ...*161*
The Story of Witold Zachanowicz ...*163*
Some Realities of Life in Eastern Europe ...*168*
Camps Begin in Croatia ...*173*
Croatian Fruit ...*176*
Chris Davies Reactivates Student Work in Hungary ...*179*
Moving On ...*185*
Will You Follow? ...*192*
References ...*200*
Notes ...*201*
Index ...*202*

Foreword by Sir Fred Catherwood

In the summer of 1969, a year after their country had been invaded by the tanks of the Warsaw Pact, a group of Czech students arrived at an old castle in Austria for an international conference. About a hundred cheerful, talkative international students filled the castle. But the Czechs waited until they were out in the forests before they dared to talk openly and when they went back home at the end we did not know whether we would ever see them again.

Over the following years small groups came each summer from other countries behind the Iron Curtain, Poles, Hungarians, Yugoslavs and in due course a few Czechs too.

All of them knew that, if they held to their faith, they would have a rough time in the army and would find it hard to get jobs in schools, universities or the public service. Yet they stuck firmly to their faith.

One Hungarian girl felt that, in applying for a job as a teacher, she had to say that she was a Christian. All her applications were turned down until, finally and unexpectedly she was asked to see a head teacher who was also the local communist party secretary. He said, "I have so many applications from people who tell me lies to get a job that I had to see someone who knew that, by telling the truth, she would not get a job." They had a long talk, at the end of which he offered her the job, so long as she did not teach Christianity. She said, "But what if they ask me what I believe?" Then, after another long discussion he put her on her honour not to talk to them about her faith unless they asked her first.

These little bands of Iron Curtain students, sixes from here and sevens from there, did not arrive by accident. Behind them was a careful organiser, Alex Williams, the author of this book, taking his freedom in his hands for the sake of the gospel.

His work has expanded twenty-fold here, a hundred-fold there. In 1994 my wife and I, who had been houseparents at the old Austrian castle, went to a conference of Christian students from all over Central and Eastern Europe, two and a half thousand jammed into a sports college in Warsaw meant to accommodate only fifteen hundred. The Polish movement alone had four hundred students. There were coaches from far away, Prague and Minsk and even Siberia.

This is the authentic story by the man who started it all, a story of the power of God behind one gentle man.

Fred Catherwood

Dedication

Many friends of the International Fellowship of Evangelical Students, IFES, from around the world, many of them graduates of Inter-Varsity related movements, gave willingly, during the 1970s so that, in those difficult days when communism ruled in Eastern Europe, Christian students could be encouraged by a visit, helped to share their faith in their residence, restaurant or room, and built up through attending a Bible conference.

This book gives an insight into how those 1970s dollars, pounds, francs and marks were used under the IFES umbrella in Eastern Europe.

This book is particularly dedicated to the staff and students associated with the International Fellowship of Evangelical Students, Oxford, England, to the URCO Foundation in Holland who generously supported me in the work, and to the Polska Ewangeliczna Misja Zagraniczna (Polish Evangelical Foreign Mission) Ustroń, Poland and to other similar missions emerging today across modern Central Europe.

My prayer is that God might use these stories to inspire students today to be faithful and courageous to serve him in their generation.

Acknowledgments

I am deeply indebted to the veritable host of kind people who have contributed to this book. Many of them allowed me to interview them, or contributed written memoirs of the exciting times we shared. You will find their names throughout the text. My son, David, generously drew the maps, and created the web pages you can find under www.holyspy.com However, the text you see would not be nearly so readable without the ministrations of Dr. Marcia Munger (of Schloss Mittersill) and Gerry Davey who have doctored my efforts with their excellent editing skills. Rachelle Thackray, Basil Bigg and Gordon Parke also helped and greatly encouraged me in earlier days, while Kirsty Thorburn of IFES very kindly revised the chapter Moving On and made other valuable suggestions.

Finally, there would be no book at all without my publisher, Dr Kornél Herjeczki and his fine team at the Harmat Publishing House in Budapest, and there would be no story to tell without my longsuffering wife, Anikó.

All the faults and mistakes are mine. I would be most grateful for help in making the next edition better.

Alex Williams,
Budapest, May 2003.

INTRODUCTION

Das Evangelium, welches der Herr
den Aposteln in den Mund gelegt hat,
ist sein Schwert.
Damit schlägt Er in die Welt,
als mit Blitz und Donner.

The Gospel, which the Lord
has put into the mouth of his apostles,
is his sword,
with which he strikes in the world
like lightning and thunder." Martin Luther

Martin Luther was called before the Reichstag, or Diät, in Worms on the Rhine in 1521. He refused to recant with the famous words, "Here I stand. I cannot do otherwise. So help me God. Amen."

We admire Martin Luther, his vision for the gospel and his steadfast work for the Lord. In 1521, pursued by his enemies, Luther's friends hid him in the Wartburg Castle near Eisenach. When I first saw the Wartburg under communism a big attraction was to peek from the ramparts over the fields and formidable fences from East into West Germany. For Luther the Wartburg was a modest refuge. In a tiny room set in the castle wall his stint for a year was to translate the entire New Testament into his mother tongue. Yet this great man, mightily used by God, also suffered tremendous doubts. The Prince of Darkness tempted him with questions. "Are you alone wise? Have so many centuries gone wrong? What if you are in error and taking so many others with you to eternal damnation?"

Then in the morning he would throw open the casement window and look out on the fair wooded Thuringian hills. He might see a cloud of smoke in the distance rising from the pits of the charcoal burners. A gust of wind would lift and dissipate the cloud, and he felt his doubts also dispelled and his faith restored.

I was called by God to contribute to building his Church in another age—during the final years of the reign of communism in Eastern Europe. Student work is very exciting and stimulating. Students are among the people in society most open to consider the claims of Jesus Christ. Generally they have not yet either hardened into cynicism or become engrossed in climbing their career ladder or supporting their family. Won for Christ they are always having fresh ideas. So they can be particularly effective and enthusiastic as Christian witnesses.

The heart of IFES, to quote its first General Secretary, Stacey Woods, writing about student work in the USA; "is on campus, in the life and service, discipleship and witness of Christian students themselves who, under divine conviction, are committed and compelled to stand for the Lord Jesus and to make him known during their undergraduate days. This is Inter-Varsity: essentially an undergraduate, student movement—of students, by students and for students. Work among graduates, faculty and all else is subsidiary to this." Growth of a Work of God, Inter-Varsity Press, 1978 page 158)

Perhaps God is calling you too. Begin where you are. Don't despise the day of small things, and if you too, like me, and like many others before us, are afflicted by doubts, look back—to Jesus who rose with mighty power from the grave. Look up to him who is calling you to work for him today, and look forward to Jesus who will strengthen you for the way ahead. If he could use me, he can use you too! In his book "No Little People" Francis Schaeffer wrote "In God's sight there are no little people and no little places. Those who think of themselves as little people in little places, if committed to Christ and living under his lordship in the whole of life, may, by God's grace, change the flow of history".

Otto von Bismarck, the great Chancellor who united Germany in the second half of the 19th century, is credited with saying that politics is the art of being in the station when the train comes in. It's an apt metaphor that fits this story. Which station should we wait in? Where and what should we do? As we set out to work for God we found that, in his goodness, he led and kept us through ten years of patient toil in Eastern Europe, often through danger to ourselves and more especially to others with whom we were involved. This is the story of how God did guide IFES, the International Fellowship of Evangelical Students, in working out his plan for Eastern Europe. So it was that for the whole of the Soviet Union, East Germany, Poland, Czechoslovakia, Hungary, Romania, Bulgaria, and Yugoslavia we were ready and in the station when the train of glasnost and perestroika came in. This openness and restructuring together with democratisation, represented a powerful trio of ideals. The present era of new freedoms arrived in 1989. Surely, without living to realise it, Stacey Woods had truly sensed the "hour of God" for IFES to begin work in Eastern Europe, when in 1969 he shared his vision with me and my wife.

Stacey was, at that time, General Secretary of the IFES. Would we be willing to travel for IFES in communist Eastern Europe? Could we, he asked, seek out Christian students, and encourage them to witness to their peers? We had questions too. Was it so dangerous that Stacey was in effect sending us into a "Lion's den"? Or was he more like Moses, sending us to spy out the promised land? There were dangers and difficulties, but the Lord saved us from them time and time again. We did "spy out the land", and when communism cracked and the Wall came down in 1989, student movements all across Eastern Europe were ready and waiting to organise formally and claim official recognition.

There had been IFES related student work in some of these countries before the Second World War, but the communists had closed it down, and many church leaders felt there was no need now for anything more than their own, often anaemic, church-related youth work. It was the pastors we had to win over to new ideas about students reaching students. They were much more suspicious than any of the students. Did we want to expose their young people to terrible capitalist sins—pornography and materialism? Would their young people ever return to Eastern Europe if they went for a Christian camp to the decadent West? And who were we? Who employed us? Why were we travelling around looking for Christian students? Almost no one knew of IFES and we did not like to explain it in case it sounded like a cover for the proscribed foreign organisation which, in fact, it was. However, it was not anti-communist, but trying to establish member movements in the communist countries, and primarily concerned to spawn effective indigenous local networks of students witnessing to their peers about their Christian faith. At that time organisations outside the actual structure of the churches were all forbidden, particularly international organisations. They had always been more open to the suspicion of being used to infiltrate agents or subvert nationals to try to upset the political status quo. Even as a post-graduate student in Poland I had been suspected by a pastor of being the "agent" of a mission—a sort of **holy spy**—though such was not at all in my mind at the time. The pastor, Alek Kircun, while being consistently friendly towards me, did not feel free to tell me of his suspicions till the communists were well and truly gone, 25 years later.

WEDDING IN HUNGARY

Many people find Europe a mystery with all its many languages, and Eastern Europe especially so. This was compounded for 45 years after the Second World War by the dominance of communism in Eastern Europe. From 1945 to 1989 its citizens were, assuredly, strange folk indeed.

I had my first contact with Eastern Europe as a student at Leeds University. Friends there called me "Ceramics Alex" after my main subject of study. As part of our Christian Union's social concern I was one of those who welcomed foreign students as they arrived, showed them around and tried to make them feel at home.

The British Council is the U.K. body which arranges many academic exchanges. When the local organiser in Leeds told me that a Polish student was coming to our tiny ceramics department I made sure I was down on the station platform to meet him. Mirosław Grylicki and I became firm friends at Leeds during 1964/65. He arranged for my first visit to Poland during the summer of 1965, which led on to my postgraduate work there from 1966—68. I visited Mirosław in his Gdańsk home one summer in the mid 1980's, and a couple of years after that he brought his wife to visit us and we engaged in numerous fungus forays. The mushrooms which appear during the autumn in the woods and meadows of Poland, as in England, are loved and sought after by the Poles. The English tend to be afraid of what they term "toadstools".

I have one particularly significant memory from that first visit to Poland in 1965. My guide and mentor at the Institute of Refractory Materials in the Upper Silesian industrial town of Gliwice was Zdźisław Librant. We quickly became good friends. I was down on my hands and knees scrubbing the floor of his flat, preparing it for painting. Barbara, his fiancée arrived, and was visibly shocked and asked me "Don' t you all have servants to do such things in England? "

How did we imagine life in Eastern Europe? How did they imagine life in the West? As you read on you will find some of the reality of life under communism. How did men and women suffer, survive and even thrive?As I tell my story, we meet real people, we hear their true stories, we see life behind the newspaper and television reports, we put faces and names on to one of the most significant and difficult times for Christians in the twentieth century.

It was in the autumn of 1967 that I entered the British Embassy in Budapest. Asking to see a consular official I enquired if there was any possibility of my marrying a Hungarian girl. "Oh yes," he assured me in a very down to earth manner. "You get married first, then there is not usually more than a few months wait before the Hungarian authorities decide if they will grant her a passport. If she gets it, come back and I will make sure she also gets the visa she will need to enter Britain."

Getting married "Behind the Iron Curtain"! I was swept off my feet and hardly realised what I was letting myself in for. Anikó Kmethy was the first Hungarian I met. It was not love at first sight, but after a lazy September day on a paddle steamer slowly making headway against the flow of the Danube from a landing stage in Budapest to Kisoroszi, a tiny village at the northernmost point of the Szentendre Island, I was done for.

Tóth József, the pastor of the Reformed church in Kisoroszi and a friend of Anikó since she was seven, was out. We sat under the verandah of his white painted house which stood next to the church on a corner of the village square and admired the well in the centre of his garden. This was not the conventional type of Hungarian "puszta" well with its long beam and weight to balance the bucket. It was a covered well with a chain to wind to let the bucket down a deep well shaft and so draw up a refreshing drink of cool fresh water.

As József was not at home, despite Anikó having sent a telegram to advise him of our visit, we wandered for five minutes through the houses and back to the landing stage. But it would be hours yet before the steamer would return on its daily run from Budapest to Esztergom and back. Now, with no one to visit, we could not face the wait. We spent time admiring the view from Kisoroszi, west across the Danube to Visegrád with the massive remains of its fine ruined castle and north towards the hills around the Danube Bend. Then across the Szentendre Island we went for a ferry to Vác, famous for its fortress-like prison in which many of Hungary's political prisoners were incarcerated.

In 1968 Anikó became my wife. Later she would be a wonderful partner for me in the work God called me to do for him in Eastern Europe. Her father had always been afraid she would marry one of those foreign students—and I was one of them. When we first met she was always helping those who arrived at her church in Nap utca (Sun Street) in downtown Budapest.

Getting married in Hungary was straightforward after all the formalities had been completed. We were married in a registry office in December 1968, and planned to have a church blessing in June the following year. However Anikó received her passport in six weeks rather than the expected six months. Her father had heard of another girl who had married a German, got her passport, and then had it withdrawn. Not wishing for a similar fate we decided to speed matters up and set the date for February 22, 1969. There was just time to invite our friends. None from England felt like braving the mid-European winter to travel to Budapest in February, but our Polish friends were not to be so easily put off.

Józef Prower, a Jew I'd met in his flat in Castle Street (ul Zamkowa) in the industrial town of Bielsko-Biała early on during two years of postgraduate studies in Poland, came with his wife. Józef, a delightful man who took me to his fruit garden and regaled me with fresh raspberries and red currants, had been converted through a scripture booklet given to him while travelling on a train in England! Later, because of a heart condition, he was not able to work and instead received a fairly generous invalidity pension. This freed him to engage in his passion, translating Christian books. But it also turned him into a thorn in the side of the authorities because of the huge volume of good Christian books he translated into Polish.

Józef translated directly into a dictating machine from both English and German. He kept a small army of typists busy and as a result a whole Christian library was published through the United Evangelical Church. Józef had been forbidden a passport, even to visit his sister in Paris. "But next time you get an invitation you will have your passport," he had been told by the officer. "Next time" was our wedding invitation. "Hallelujah, coming!" his telegram announced. Józef's heart condition caught up with him a few years later. His wife found him dead one morning, sitting with the book open from which he had been translating the night before. He would have wished for no better way to go.

Our student friends were also under pressure from the authorities, as almost all active Christians were at that time. Withholding a passport was common, as was pressure to inform at a debriefing session on return from abroad. Weddings and funerals were perhaps the best reason to apply for a passport, and the least likely to be refused. Nelek and Jan Wojnar, two other Polish friends, arrived with their violin and cello, and together with Józef Prower they entertained us at our wedding breakfast.

The day after the wedding we left Budapest by train. "We" included George Thackray, my friend from college days in Leeds who had been my best man. George and I had taken transit visas as these were free of compulsory currency exchange, but the Hungarian border guard was not going to let us "change our minds" and return to Austria. Ulla Bella Engelbrektson, a tall and vivacious blonde Swedish girl who was working with Operation Mobilisation in Vienna advised us to say, when challenged, that we had changed our minds. She was quite adept at "changing her mind" and getting away with it. Did that sometimes help, we wondered, if she told this to customs officers when smuggling Bibles and other Christian literature? It was widely suspected that Operation Mobilisation did engage in smuggling Christian literature.

Somehow two young innocent Englishmen did not similarly impress the border guard. So from the Hungarian/Austrian border at Hegyeshalom, George and I went by slow train to Komárom, half way back to Budapest, where we could cross the River Danube on foot over the bridge to Komárno on the Slovak side—and catch an even slower train to Bratislava. Meanwhile Anikó sped on alone from Hegyeshalom to Vienna in the Wiener Walzer Express.

Our Slovak train featured central heating of a type I have never seen before or since. A basket of coal hung next to a stove located in the centre of our carriage. The conductor periodically arrived to check tickets, and as he passed took a shovel full of coal from the basket to feed the stove. Too near to the stove and you were too hot, too far away and you were too cold. We found a happy medium, and devoured home made smoked Hungarian sausages for our impromptu picnic. These were a wedding present intended to be savoured over many months spicing up many different Hungarian dishes in England, not eaten in one meal!

George prepared a Bible study, and eventually we arrived at the terminus on the outskirts of Bratislava. From there we travelled on by taxi to the Austrian border. We had just missed the evening train connection to Vienna, and the bus had also left. Hitching a lift did not work out, so we phoned to our dear friend Ulla Bella, as she it was who had landed us in this mess.

"Oh, yes, we will send someone to collect you," she told us from Operation Mobilisation's headquarters. They did, much later in the evening, and in true O.M. fashion distributed tracts to all the Austrian border guards! We eventually arrived, well after midnight, back at OM's Vienna base.

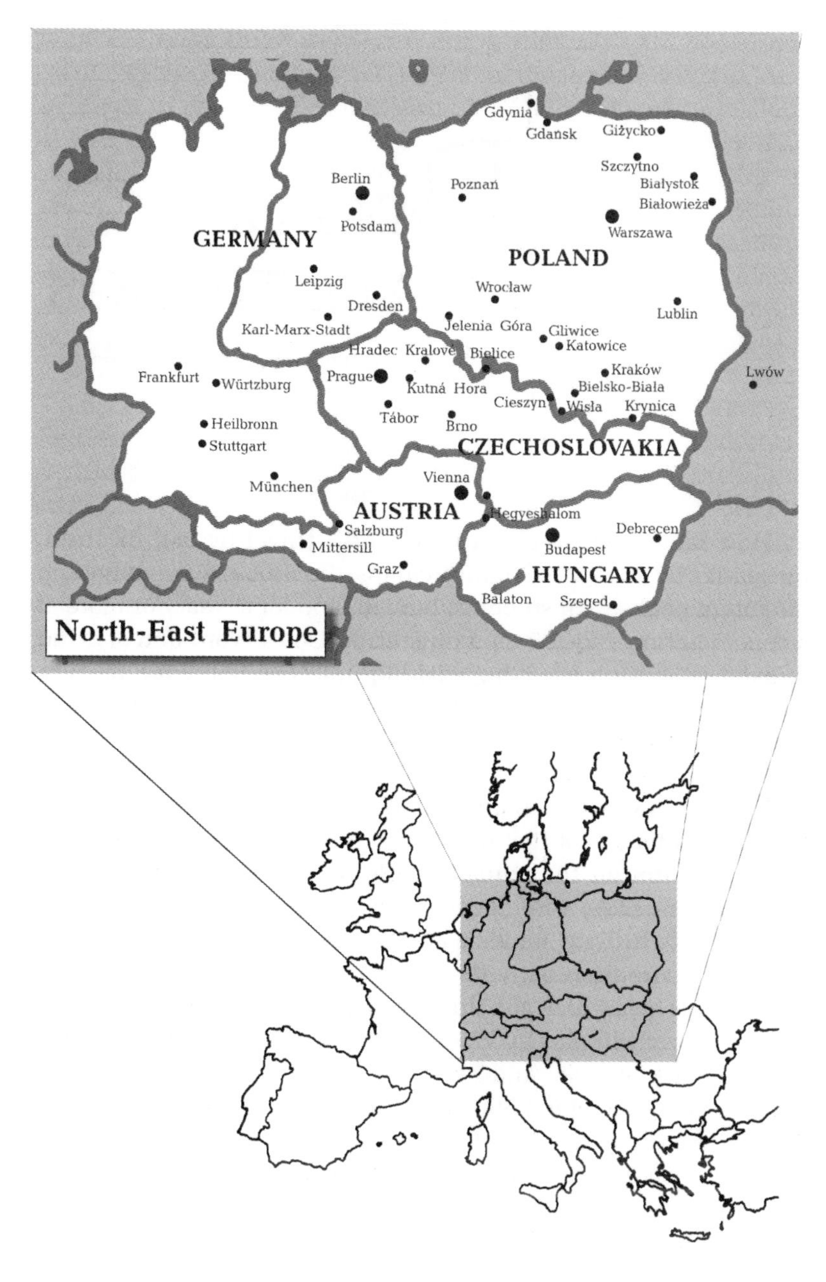
North-East Europe
GERMANY
POLAND
CZECHOSLOVAKIA
AUSTRIA
HUNGARY
Gdynia
Gdańsk
Giżycko
Szczytno
Białystok
Białowieża
Poznań
Berlin
Potsdam
Warszawa
Leipzig
Wrocław
Dresden
Lublin
Karl-Marx-Stadt
Jelenia Góra
Gliwice
Katowice
Hradec Kralové
Bielice
Frankfurt
Würtzburg
Prague
Kutná Hora
Kraków
Bielsko-Biała
Lwów
Cieszyn
Wisła
Krynica
Tábor
Brno
Heilbronn
Stuttgart
München
Vienna
Hegyeshalom
Salzburg
Mittersill
Debrecen
Budapest
Graz
Balaton
Szeged

DAYS OF SMALL THINGS

How many thousands of miles did I travel by car, by train, by plane, by bus! How many camps did I share in—climbing mountain peaks with students, buying food for seventy or more at a time, peeling vegetables, ministering God's Word and sharing relaxed fellowship over the washing up! How many tea parties, suppers and coffees have I taken to share not only physical food, but more importantly spiritual encouragement!

It was a wonderful privilege to be a member of the field staff of IFES. For ten years I laboured alongside men and women with a huge vision for a task that under our great God we would attempt together, winning the student world for Christ! What could be more exciting? We were commissioned with enormous measures of freedom to be with students and sometimes share their sorrows, but much more frequently their joys.

I did not even look for this job. Late in autumn 1969, I was invited to apply by Stacey Woods, an Australian from the outback who was at that time, and had been since its inception in 1947, IFES General Secretary. Stacey was an enigmatic yet inspirational man with a great love for life which I was to find infectious, and which was shared to a large degree by most of the other staff.

We soon realized that IFES was being run on a shoe-string. We didn't know it then, but have since come to appreciate that most mission work is just the same. Money can be a double-edged tool. It can certainly serve the needs, but either too little or too much could lead to inefficiency or waste in our Christian work. Perhaps the most frequently repeated of Stacey Woods' slogans regarding IFES work was never to despise the days of small things.

The Apostle Paul really knew what he was talking about. "Although saddened, we are always glad; we seem poor, but we make many people rich" (2 Cor 6:10). Surely still today it is better to be rich in faith and poor in money rather than to be rich in money and poor in faith.

"God chose the poor people of this world to be rich in faith and to possess the kingdom which he promised to those who love him" (James 2:5). The vision for what can be done, what absolutely needs to be done, is almost always running ahead of the funds available. "With all his abundant wealth through Christ Jesus, my God will supply all your needs" (Phil. 4:19). All your needs—maybe not all your wants or dreams! Some years all field operations had to stop when funds ran low in the autumn, but good people always gave again so that, if we slowed down during October and November, we could probably run a Christmas/New Year house party—provided our bill for expenses was not sent in until January.

For missionaries, enthusiasm for the task in hand is so great that they are almost always struggling to make ends meet. That is a special problem when, as they do, the ends keep moving. Stacey Woods experienced the same times of testing himself as a young staff worker in the United States. He describes it charmingly in his book *Some Ways of God:*

"In the early days of Inter-Varsity when income was small and uncertain, every staff member, I think, had similar experiences. I remember one Sunday in San Francisco. Student visits in Oakland, the Bay Area and the Peninsula were finished. I had less than a dollar in my pocket—insufficient to continue south and east—and San Francisco is not a particularly hospitable city. I went to a local church for the morning service. Later I discovered my father had ministered there in evangelism for some weeks, but I knew no one. After the service a family invited me home for dinner, then to spend

the rest of the day and that night with them. As I left the next morning my host pressed $50 into my hand. So I went on my way rejoicing and praising God."

"Sometimes I feel that Christian workers who have never been up against it physically and materially nor seen God work miraculously, though through human channels, have missed an exciting and wonderful blessing. We should remember that living by complete trust in God is God's mandate for every Christian, not just for the exceptional Christian."

Stacey's words still ring in my ears. We were certainly in no danger of missing such exciting and wonderful blessings! Stacey Woods was wonderful at sharing his vision with supporters across the world, particularly those in North America. He had been General Secretary of Canadian Inter-Varsity, and later he had founded Inter-Varsity, the IFES-related student movement, in the USA. Here he had lots of friends who understood the needs of the pioneering work. He gave himself to it with unstinting energy—and naturally inspired all his staff to do likewise.

Later when Stacey came to know some rich people, conditions changed remarkably, and he described his "hilarious days":

"Through W.E. Weyerhaeuser I had free first-class rail passes on the Great Northern and the North Pacific railways, and at his insistence, full of self-consciousness and embarrassment, I would ride to the student union at the University of Minnesota or to Macalester College or St. Olaf's in a Cadillac driven by a chauffeur. To the wide-eyed amazement of the students, the chauffeur would open the car door, and I would step out into the student union for an Inter-Varsity meeting."[1]

I doubt if, in 1970 when I joined the staff, Stacey was consciously aiming at an ultimate goal in Eastern Europe. Stacey was concerned that we should just live each day for the Lord. Only God knew that by 1989 the Berlin Wall would be coming down, and that by 1994 even the communists in the Russian parliament would be reduced to a minority party. But though there was never a grand design announced which, for example, would see the formation of a worldwide IFES by the year 1990 or 2000, we certainly had an intermediate goal, the establishment of self-supporting independent student movements in all the East European countries. Such was the blessing and success of our work that, under God the great designer, many movements were indeed ready to spring into independent registered existence right across Eastern Europe immediately they were officially allowed to do so.

However, that was all a long way off. Having invited me to apply to join his staff Stacey decided that we could give it a go for one year only, and should remain based in our little rented cottage at Newick in Sussex, southern England. Our next door neighbour, the faithful village pastor Gordon Diamond, told us later that he and his wife, who we nicknamed 'Double Diamond' prayed for us every day. What a wonderful gift, to have supporters like that. We all need them! Just as wonderful a support was that IFES would be responsible for the rent. This was also less disruptive for us and cheaper for IFES than anywhere else in the whole of Western Europe. We are still in our little rented cottage to this day thirty or so years later. In fact, over the years it has proved to be a God-given place to make our home, our nest, and bring up our children. Shaded by tall trees, the bird life is rich and varied while it is only a stone's throw from the post office, and the village bakery. More importantly it is not too ostentatious whenever we have wanted to welcome any visitor from even the poorest part of Eastern Europe. It is truly a God given retreat from the hectic world of bustling cities full of trams and trains, shops and students.

Stacey invited Anikó and me to call on him in Lausanne, Switzerland, before we set off to pay our first visit East. Early in January 1970, we loaded up our little Mini van and booked an overnight channel crossing. Ours was one of only four cars on the trip from Dover to Calais. The ferry was a tiny one by today's standards and accommodation was basic. No cabin, just a partition to separate us from other sleepy travellers. The boat was more of a youth hostel than a floating hotel.

By 2 a.m. we were driving across France. Our knowledge of French was so basic that we didn't care to stop. The weather was atrocious and to make matters worse I had looked at a map of

Europe and had just drawn a line across the shortest route from Calais to Lausanne. This did not take any account of mountain passes! We avoided them on later trips, but on this trip I vividly recall the car skidding while descending a snowy pass after we had crossed into Switzerland. We slid round a metal road barrier, but were fortunately none the worse for wear. Not even the paint was scratched!

We must have looked mighty tired when we arrived in Lausanne. Yvonne Woods, Stacey's charming Canadian wife, fed us magnificently and put us to bed. The next day, after prayers over Stacey's burnt toast—we never did come to understand why he enjoyed this culinary delicacy so much—it was down to the offices of the grandly named International Fellowship of Evangelical Students. These consisted of a paltry two or three rooms on a single floor in an ordinary house rented from a charming old man in the church the Woods attended. The old boy lived downstairs, and the IFES was upstairs. Stacey was in one room, with Jennifer, his truly efficient English multilingual secretary, in the lobby. Another room housed the theological secretary, an American going by the very fine name of the Reverend Dr Harold O Joe Brown. To complete the staff were Dr Brown's skilful Swiss multilingual secretary, Erna Kull, and Mitzi the Italian accountant who must also have been multilingual in currency. She paid staff all over the world in dozens of currencies and received gifts and subscriptions in even more.

That then was the tiny office support staff, but did that Lausanne office buzz! Glass partitions divided the rooms, which created a sense of urgency, of a team working together, of a movement on the move—very different from a normal office, in an inflexible building which so easily locks its inhabitants into cell-like cubicles behind solid wooden doors.

Stacey used to walk down the hill, about thirty minutes to the office each morning, and take the tram back up in time for lunch, the Swiss noon meal. Then he'd walk back down again in the afternoon, assuming, of course, that he was not on one of his frequent journeys to supporters, mainly in North America, or away on a trip to encourage students and staff in one of the far-flung corners of the world. Stacey told me that, as he walked, he prayed. He prayed for IFES staff for an hour each day. No wonder he could offer helpful advice and insights into different people's situations when they met.

Stacey ' s habit of prayer was a great lesson for me. As I developed the work in Eastern Europe I would jog for around an hour every day when at home in England. It could have looked to passers-by like a complete waste of time—apart from taking the air and having some exercise—but those who noticed me would never know I was interceding to God for all those I worked with.

Looking back it seems rather funny, but at the time we were just so thankful to God that we had arrived safely in Lausanne. Our little British Mini van was soon to be recognised by students and friends all over Eastern Europe. Even in some of the remotest towns in Romania or Hungary they would come rushing to see us, telling us that they had spotted us in town or visiting someone else, but that they were sure we would soon be making a call on them. But for now our van had had enough. It took us up the hill on the edge of Lausanne to Stacey's house—yet refused to budge at all the following day. We looked out, back down towards the town, and to our amazement there was a garage about 100 yards down the hill. I free-wheeled the car back down the hill to the garage. They soon diagnosed the trouble. The fuel pump needed replacing, and it would take a week to obtain the part. Was this the way God saved us from much worse trouble if we had continued, as planned, to travel on immediately by car through snow and ice into Eastern Europe?

In the event, my first journey east for IFES was by train from Lausanne while the garage obtained and fitted the new pump. Stacey knew the best trains well. He and Dr. Hans Bürki, the Swiss IFES Associate General Secretary-at-Large who very wisely worked from his Lenzburg home, travelled by train whenever possible. It made a lot of sense. You could read and study, eat and sleep while travelling. When you arrived you were rested, and much less noticeable than if you had travelled in a foreign car. You would, if necessary, wait till evening for the cover of darkness before making sensitive visits. But even then you'd walk or take a taxi, not to the address, but to a neighbouring street.

INSIDE THE WEIRD WORLD OF EASTERN EUROPE

State authorities in Eastern Europe were strict with Christian people at this time. They feared alien propaganda being brought in from the West, and churches were the only bodies allowed to function which were not under the direct control of the communist party or the state apparatus. No wonder the authorities were apprehensive of what might be going on and of what they plainly, as avowed atheists and materialists, did not understand. This often led to the repression of Christianity.

There was always the very real fear of repercussions on those we visited, probably in the form of being summoned or visited by the secret police for questioning. Pastors were under an obligation to inform the secret police on Monday morning if any foreigner had been in their congregation on Sunday. Certain friends in Romania lost their whole library of Christian books when the secret police, the dreaded Securitate, called on one occasion and made a particularly thorough search. Knowing that this could happen, the Christians had previously taken the precaution of hiding the books under the floorboards! In the event it did not help; they showed me a receipt for their confiscated library.

"We were singing from the new song book you so kindly brought, when the Securitate arrived." Timotei told me later. "They searched everywhere and confiscated all our precious books, illegally smuggled Western propaganda that would do us no good, they told us."

As we travelled east we sometimes took good Christian books along to strengthen folk spiritually or to give solid Bible teaching to those who were leaders in their church youth group or music group. If we managed to get them into the country we didn't want to arouse any suspicions by leaving our car anywhere near our friend's home. Even arriving outside the home of Christian people during the hours of daylight could be dangerous. A prying neighbour could receive a handsome reward for reporting that Christians had received a visit from the West. For the safety of those you set out to help no foreign car could be safely parked anywhere near a Christian leader's home or outside any student residence. We always committed names and addresses to memory so that friends would not be compromised if the border guards decided, as they actually would on frequent occasions, to go through all our belongings with a fine toothed comb. We could sight-see like ordinary tourists during the mornings and afternoons, then rest, and so be prepared for the main business of the day when the students were free and at home in the evenings.

Border controls were an occupational hazard in our work. I dreaded them. They generally lasted for around an hour, but could easily drag on for four hours or more, even after you arrived at the front of the queue. Despite their regularity and inevitability there is something humiliating and embarrassing, almost degrading, about having your privacy invaded by a rough and determined customs officer. He or she would proceed by searching your wash-bag, looking inside your ties, handling all your underclothes, rifling your briefcase or unscrewing the dash-board inside the car, taking x-ray pictures of the tyres, using mirrors to look under your car, turning out your pockets or smelling inside your socks in a cold-blooded and at the same time frenzied search for goods which today would not attract the slightest attention. The East Germans were the most regularly thorough. The Romanians were the worst if they decided to strike, which they usually did, and the Czechoslovaks came in a close third!

Only once did I have the attentions of the Polish "Black Brigade", and then there was a genuinely good cause. I was travelling from Gdynia, on the Baltic coast, to London by boat, a British ship on a regular run. I had passed customs on entering the dock area earlier in the afternoon. Now the ship was loaded and the captain wanted to sail but in the meantime three customs officers had arrived and were systematically checking through my every neck-tie, to say nothing of all my other belongings. Eventually they agreed they could find nothing untoward, and we sailed for London, but a week or so later I happened to hear in a BBC radio news bulletin that Polish customs had picked up this ship's radio officer. He was charged with smuggling industrial diamonds!

On another occasion I was wonderfully saved from a search at the Hungarian border, although through this event I was refused a visa to enter Hungary for over a year afterwards. I was in my car at Sopron, waiting to pass through customs. The officer told me to drive into the special large garage at the side of the road where particularly thorough searches were made in privacy, when the motorist behind me alerted me to the fact that I had a flat tyre. I stopped the car and got out to look. Sure enough, it was flat. Then, glancing back towards Austria I noticed the big yellow sign of the Austrian motor club, ÖAMTC.

"Could I please go back to get help for my puncture?" The customs officer glared, but could hardly refuse. I was so nearly in his grasp. He was furious, and later it became obvious that he had at that moment put me on the "Black List" of people to be forbidden entry. He was not to know that in fact I had nothing to hide. It was more than a nuisance to be refused access, and I had to request the Hungarian authorities through the British Embassy to be struck off their "Black List". In due course they had mercy and relented.

East European currencies were simply amazing at this time—very wacky indeed. Western businessmen were obliged, by law, to use a very unfavourable rate of exchange, because the socialist states were in desperate need of hard (western) currency. Perhaps it was also to restrict trade with the evil capitalist West. Tourists received a "premium", in many cases greater than 100% over the official business rate. But there was just one snag—you had to change quite a generous set amount per day. This was designed to cut down on the free exchange of currency. If, as a tourist, you had as much as you could reasonably expect to spend on a hotel and meals, there was no great incentive to change more money. However, the demand for hard currency always exceeded the supply. Ordinary East Europeans who wanted to travel out to the West were allocated paltry sums of just a few dollars for their immediate travel needs.Those who invited them were expected to pick up the tab for all their expenses and their fares as well in many cases.

The authorities recognised this, and allowed for the fact that their people would somehow acquire hard currency. If East Europeans took dollars, francs or pounds to the bank they would be rewarded by yet a higher rate than the foreign tourist could obtain. It was certainly not unknown for foreign tourists in the know to ask their East European friends to change money for them at the bank. Finally there was what was known in the West as the free rate, and in the East as the black market rate which would often be five or six times the normal "tourist" rate. But once you had changed your unnecessarily generous quota at the decidedly less than generous official rate, did you need more money? Could you even find worthwhile items to buy?

The banks in Vienna, so it was rumoured, received ample supplies of Czech crowns, Hungarian forints, and Polish złoty etc. from the respective embassies, who brought it out in their diplomatic bags. Certainly some funds also came out with ordinary East Europeans, but they generally earned so little that it would certainly appear to them that they received an abominable rate of exchange. However, Westerners travelling into Eastern Europe could stock up with local currencies extremely cheaply. There was only one snag. It was illegal to either export or import Polish money, and the same went for the other countries. Not surprisingly other customs laws were also pretty strict regarding what you could export.

If currency was a charade, so were many other parts of East European life. Andrzej Wajda's famous film "Man of Iron", portraying the rise of Solidarity in the Lenin shipyard at Gdańsk, was preceded by "Man of Marble" in which worker heroes are seen building the industrial suburb of Cracow called Nowa Huta. It was an empty show. The hollowness, the falseness of the communist system was shown. Hero builders were supplied with blocks of marble and other materials by large teams of their mates to enable them to achieve superhuman accomplishments. I was not the only one to be amazed that such a film could pass the Polish censor, but it did.

Georges Remi cleverly showed the same sham in his 1930 "Tintin in the Soviet Union". Tintin watches a group of English communists admiring the pace of post-revolutionary progress at a factory apparently in full swing. But he soon discovers that the impressive smoke and noise of industrial production is being created by two workers burning hay and banging a sheet of metal with a hammer. The film is only slightly exaggerated. Tintin witnesses a 'democratic' election, in which communist officials seek support from a crowd, and then out come their guns before asking if anyone wants to vote against them. Food is being stolen, there is appalling neglect, poverty and intimidation in the ordinary streets of Moscow—away from the tourist sights—and such scenes are set against others showing revolutionary leaders amassing secret hordes of wealth, and of food supposedly destined for export to give the impression of the Soviet economic miracle to the West.

Europe has a good rail system, and during my ten years with IFES I travelled much of the network. It was a far cry from our local Brighton Belle of cherished memory—a train with elegantly dressed waiters, individually crafted seats, and deeply polished tables. On the Brighton Belle you partook of delicate cucumber sandwiches with afternoon tea and cream cakes from a silver service, enjoying the rolling Sussex countryside through picture windows on both sides of the carriage. In Eastern Europe trains were usually slow, often dirty, the windows typically grimy or misted. Carriages were either overheated or freezing cold in winter. However there were some 1930s carriages still in service, carriages with sumptuous first class, and bone shaking third class compartments! Gradually these were being replaced by more proletarian wagons fitted with less than super first class, and hard plastic second class seats. It was usually best to take plenty of your own provisions for the journey as the buffet, if one existed, could quickly be reduced to beer only. And while trains were almost always late by an hour or more, they were very convenient. Trains do go between cities, and to the city centres; exactly where the students are.

While studying in Poland I once travelled by train with Dr. Hans Bürki from Warsaw to Białystok, a journey of not more than a couple of hours. Dr. Bürki, a rather large and very affable man, regaled me with the exciting and romantic story of how he met his Hungarian wife, Ágó, at a student conference. She had sat behind him but he was so intrigued with a fascinating question she put to the speaker that he determined to speak to her after the lecture.

At the time there had been an unfortunate misunderstanding about the date of Dr. Bürki's arrival in Warsaw. I was studying in the southern Polish city of Cracow and had agreed to go up to Warsaw to meet him and escort him round the country to the various towns where I had been able, through contacts, to arrange for students to meet him, or to gather their friends to hear him preach the Gospel. Dr. Bürki told me the day he would be travelling to Warsaw. I assumed, wrongly as it turned out, that the date he gave me was the date the train departed from Vienna. He arrived in Warsaw, and I was nowhere to be seen. He did not know that I had booked him in to stay at a church guest-house in the capital, so he took a taxi to Hotel Bristol. The next day I somehow did manage to meet up with him. The dear man forgave me for my confusion. He had managed to avoid the hotel's 'ladies of the night', and when I had installed him in the church guest-house as booked, he chatted to the great and good members of various central Warsaw churches.

Hans Bürki was just one of the people I worked with during those years, all of whom showed amazing dedication to the work God had, under Stacey, given them to do. They shared Stacey's burning vision to win students, the leaders of tomorrow's world, for Christ. IFES did not have a motto, but it could have been 'win a country's students today, and the heart of that country will be set to follow Christ's way in the next generation.' They had seen this happen, dramatically in Singapore where a prime minister came from the ranks of the Christian Unions. Also many West European democracies then had people in government and as leaders of their professions who had been won for Christ while they were students.

Bob Horn, when General Secretary of the British student movement known as the Universities and Colleges Christian Fellowship, writing in "NB", a magazine for their supporters in Oct/Nov 1995, had the same vision for Ethiopia. The membership of the Evangelical Students Union of Ethiopia was almost 20% of the student population. "If 20% of the academically top one per cent are Christians, what effect could they have under God on their country in the next 30 years?" he asks. The same could happen too in every East European country. Our aim was to mobilise the Christian students to be witnesses to their peers. This was not always easy as the majority of them lived at home, and were generally heavily involved in their local churches. The local church can claim almost all of its members' spare time.

"Sunday School, two services on Sunday, young people's society, choir practice, midweek meeting, a week night Bible study, as well as many other church activities—these must have priority. The concept that a Christian student should be regarded as a missionary on a secular campus and that campus evangelism is of strategic importance comes hard. Often students unwillingly were forced to make a choice between church and campus."[2]

We faced this issue in particular with pastors of smaller free churches in Hungary, Poland and Yugoslavia. Our solution was to encourage the students to attend their churches, and to discourage Sunday student meetings. In the end there were many examples of understanding and encouragement. Students were prayed for and their outreach to their fellows supported. Now many of the students we worked with have entered church ministry, and naturally understand and support today's students in their mission. Others have entered other walks of life, and are influential there. This shows that to be a witness for Christ in the secular university milieu as an undergraduate is one of the best forms of training for effective witness in a business or professional career. "The aim of Inter-Varsity was not to remove a student from the university and its life and to imprison him in some sacrosanct ivory tower or holy huddle. It was to encourage him to be positive, outgoing, self-giving in witness to Christ and to be thereby an active, contributing member of the university community."[3]

Stacey Woods again,[4] *"It is essential to have in mind that we are not earthly, organizational empire builders. Rather we are a small part of all that Christ is doing in building his church. There is the great edifice of the church of the Lord Jesus which he is completing. All around the building is a scaffolding, a thousand different movements and organizations are on this scaffolding at different places and at different heights, each making its contribution."*

"The way to fellowship and cooperation is to realize that Christ is the great master builder. He has the eternal blueprint. We have a tiny section of it and are carrying on faithfully for him. But our section of the building is only a very tiny part of the total. Once the building is complete, all the scaffolding will be removed. None of our organizations or denominations will continue."

CRUMBLING COMMUNISM

Towards the end of 1996 it was university students who formed a large part of the daily "Zajedno" (Unity) marches in Belgrade pressing for the reinstatement of opposition wins in the November 11th elections. In 1989, it was students, including Christian students, who were at the forefront of Czechoslovakia's "Velvet Revolution". In the same way, a few months earlier, the Church had become the cradle of the people movement which resulted in the overthrow of the communist regime in East Germany. A very visible cradle it was too as, Monday after Monday, crowds gathered in a huge church in the centre of Leipzig before pouring out in their thousands through the streets to protest "We ARE the people" to the leaders of their so-called "People's Democracy".

It was a euphoric and emotional time. Although most East European countries had felt the occasional hiccup over communism, Hungary with a brave attempt at a counter-revolution in 1956, Czechoslovakia with Dubček's "Prague Spring" in 1968 etc., the dramatic collapse was unimaginable even six months before it happened. The dreary prison which communism had produced revealed itself to be no more secure than a house of cards. I felt greatly privileged to share personally in the mass euphoria bordering on delirious joy. Returning to Berlin by car with Rob Parsons and Stephen Williams, my good friends from "Care for the Family" after a fun evangelistic ski camp in Poland in February 1990, we took the road directly into the centre of the city. This was not the usually allowed route. Normally one had to follow the autobahn right round the southern half of Berlin, and enter from Drewitz, near Potsdam. But we arrived on the East Berlin side of Checkpoint Charlie. I had been quite afraid we'd be turned back, but the chief immigration officer was coming to terms with the new order. I have a memorable stamp in my passport, the very last East German one I would ever be given, with the words Friedrichstraße/Zimmerstraße.

In sharp contrast to earlier days huge floods of traffic were now passing without any attempt by the authorities to check anyone very closely. We parked close to the Checkpoint Charlie museum and walked along the wall. It was, of course, still standing, but individuals had been having a go at breaking it down with various tools. We found a crowbar which had been used and discarded. It was a wonderfully satisfying feeling to hack a hunk of concrete off that symbol of hatred and repression. To those growing up in East Germany in the years between 1961 when the Wall was built, and 1989 when it was breached, it often felt as if their whole country was a concentration camp, the purpose of which was to block off Poland and to keep under a tight rein the more obvious longings for freedom which were expressed, first from time to time by workers' demonstrations, and finally by the Polish Solidarity movement. The free trade union Solidarity grew out of Gdańsk shipyard strikes in the summer of 1980. Karol Wojtyła, Archbishop of Cracow, had been elected Pope John-Paul II in 1978. When he returned to Poland for his first visit in the summer of 1979 vast numbers flocked to hear him. The Polish Pope's appeal threatened the communist system of slavery and very soon the result was Solidarity. This movement was recognised by Polish State representatives in the historic agreement of 31st August—it was the point of conception rather than the birth of a new Poland, of new hope for the enslaved nations of Eastern Europe.

History in Eastern Europe was dangerous. Like all history, it is a record of successive struggles for power, and to a very large extent power consists in the ability to make others inhabit your story of their reality—even if, as so often is the case, that story is written in their blood. Archives were not open at all. Communist ideas were largely framed as opposing negatives. The East was what the West was not, and vice versa. So the West was characterised as dangerous and decadent—obviously the East was neither!

Even the Conference on Human Rights in Helsinki in August 1965, which 'guaranteed' freedom to travel, freedom to meet and to live without interference at home—making life rather more tolerable for Poles, Czechoslovaks and Hungarians— brought little respite to the long-suffering and repressed East Germans. In the DDR (East Germany) changes were slight and grudgingly given. Certainly no travel to the West—until you were an East German pensioner. No wonder granny's trips over the border were red letter days for all the family. She could come back with good coffee, chewing gum, bananas and maybe even a pair of jeans. Every family counted on its granny!

After 1965 travel restrictions did ease between the East European countries, and with considerable difficulties some could occasionally get to the West. But the citizens of the German Democratic Republic, the DDR, Deutsche Demokratische Republik or "Der doofe Rest" ('the stupid remainder', as some brave souls referred to their country's initials) enjoyed no such freedom.

What could, and frequently did, happen was that an East German would try to arrange to meet a West German friend or relation in another East European country, in an effort to avoid the all-searching gaze of the Stasi, the East German secret police, who virtually ran the country. A good idea? Maybe, but it often happened that letters were opened or, when an East German asked for a passport, even one for Hungary or Czechoslovakia, there would be an interview with a Stasi officer.

"Yes, you can have your passport, but we will need a report from you on your return," they would say. There would be one report, then another de-briefing session, and another, and all too soon a further unwilling co-operator had been pressed to help the

Stasi. Some people even believed that the best way for them to help to improve their country's lot would be to co-operate willingly with the Stasi. They succeeded in recruiting near on half of the entire population to work for them, spying on their fellow citizens, in some capacity.

Yet even the most rigid and brutal secret police regime could not entirely control the minds of most of their people. By day you would wear your communist badge—'Free German Youth' or 'German-Soviet Friendship Society' or even the Communist Party—but when you got home in the evenings things were very different. Then the population "fled" to the West. West German Television—either from West Berlin or from West Germany—was available to most, while radio reached the whole population. You were strictly forbidden to listen, of course, and the RIAS 'Rundfunk im amerikanischen Sektor' the American Sector Radio, was portrayed as spreading RIAS "Enten", literally "ducks", metaphorically rumours and illusions. Of course, for the poor folk living in East Germany a diet of West German television soap operas was exactly that, an illusion of real life in the West. Yet even so the vast majority of the people found such forbidden fruit, lies and deceit as their authorities called it, even more desirable than Eve found the apple in the Garden of Eden.

"Our current existence would be unthinkable without the events of May, 1945," writes a local guide to Erfurt in East Germany in 1986. "Through her act of liberation, the Soviet Union paved the way for the future happiness of our people, and from this historic deed there arose an indestructible friendship. Shoulder to shoulder with the Soviet Army, we are reliably defending peace and socialism... One thing has to be mentioned—and it is a feeling shared by all the sectors and workforces as well as by the people as a whole—and that is the close ties of friendship between our nation and the land of Lenin.."

A vigorous totalitarian order requires that the people be invested in the leader' s scheme. The spectre of an absolute menace that requires absolute eradication binds leader and people in a tightly-sealed utopian embrace, and the individual—always an annoyance to totality—ceases to exist.

The myth propagated, that East Germany was simply the best, was blatantly shattered in 1989 when the Wall came down, not only revealing the corrupt Stasi regime but also showing that the best industrial regime in Eastern Europe had been starved of real investment and was creaking along on largely pre-1939 machinery, hopelessly inefficient and polluting. Huge piles of industrial waste machinery were all too soon on view, along with broken concrete from the four metre high 'Anti-fascist ramparts', the walls around West Berlin and between East and West Germany which had been thrown up in 1961 with the claim that they were to keep out the fascists and imperialists from West Germany, but which in fact were devised to stem the brain drain from East to West Germany.

Before the Wall went up everyone who was educated knew they only had to take the train to West Berlin, present themselves along with their degree or diploma, and they would immediately have an excellent job in a thriving economy. In the East all apartments now belonged to the State, with miniscule rents for all. Bread was so cheap that it was more economical to buy bread to feed your pigs rather than proper animal feed. Fuel was so cheap that there was no point in paying for thermostats. You just opened the windows in winter to reduce the temperature. It could not last. No wonder the Wall seemed the perfect solution in 1961. It guaranteed isolation, separation of the capitalist West from the communist East.

Between the division of Germany after the Second World War by the allies, the establishment of the German Democratic Republic in the former Soviet Zone in 1948, and the erection of the Wall in 1961, 4 million East Germans had already escaped to the West out of a population of 16 million. That was despite, or perhaps because of, having 450,000 Soviet soldiers stationed on their territory.

They needed the wall to stem the tide of humanity draining away and to allow the creation of a "clean state". This allowed the perpetuation of the pantomime without the thought of any happy ending. There were no proper cars, only the Trabants (Trabis) for which you had to pay in advance and then wait up to ten years for delivery. They ran on a two stroke engine—much like that which more commonly powers a motor mower—which was reliable but very noisy and slow. When you went to order and pay in advance for your dream car you would also be given, it was said, your delivery date—ten years ahead, say, on a particular Friday. The joke was that you would look in your diary to check if you'd be free to collect your car, your prize, only to find that you had already booked that date for the plumber to call!

The Stasi were all pervasive, making as sure as possible, by having everyone watch everyone else with fearful German thoroughness, that you had the right directions, the right thoughts, the right contacts and relationships. They ruled by fear. The press would only use the expressions that were employed, and so authorised, by the leadership. The hand-picked, communist nominated leaders were Walter Ulbricht's clique, his thirteen headed gerontocracy. They ruled from April 19, 1946, when all the political parties were united into one block. Later the Communist Party was headed up by Erich Honecker, who had been leader of the so called 'Free German Youth'. Early on that government admitted that what they did "doesn't need to be democratic; it just has to look democratic". So, in the same perverse way, they gladly contributed tanks in acts of so-called 'brotherly help' along with the other Pact countries led by the Soviet Union to put down the uprisings of 1956 in Hungary and of 1968 in Czechoslovakia.

No happy ending had been planned at all for this hideous pantomime which began on April 30 1945, as Eva Braun and Adolf Hitler committed suicide. Before their bodies were cold, Ulbricht's clique flew in to Berlin from Moscow. During the years that followed, particularly 1945-47, the Red Army exploited the areas they had "liberated" throughout Eastern Europe like conquered countries held under their iron fist.

Poland followed a similar pattern. On 22 July, 1944 the Polish Committee of National Liberation, also known as the Lublin Committee, had been formed under Soviet auspices in Lublin. It assisted its Soviet masters in administering the Polish lands liberated from German occupation and in due course formed the core of Poland's communist government. Then Stalin's reign of terror rose and grew ever more fearful. There was a yearning for freedom at the heart of the postwar revolts in Poland in 1956, 1968, 1970,

1976 and most notably in 1980 when the result was the formation of the free trade union "Solidarity".

I heard a testimony by a member of the Gdańsk shipyard management team which gave a unique view of the famous strikes on the Baltic coast in August 1980 before Solidarity was formed. "I remember December 1970. So many innocent people died. There was a change at the top. The new Party bosses promised much—in turn they demanded better productivity. People believed the new leaders and their promises...then they lost their trust in them and revolted again in 1976. Those who went on strike were later persecuted, arrested and intimidated. People waited in hope of change until they could wait no more and in 1980 an 'explosion' occurred. Poles stood up to fight for social justice, to defend human dignity. It was at this time that crosses were erected at our plants. Solidarity with Christ, who died for our salvation on the cross, was growing...and it was to him that the striking Poles turned for help." Those monumental crosses outside the Baltic shipyards, emblazoned as they are with Bible texts, are yet mighty memorials to faith fighting for justice.

But in 1986 along came God's man for the hour, Mikhail Gorbachev. Arriving in Paris, playing the unlikely role of good fairy and waving his wand, he declared that no longer would the Soviet Army be used for such 'brotherly help'! Western leaders were sceptical. It sounded too good to be true. We had been imbued with slogans such as "Marxism-Leninism will triumph because it is true". Yet the celebrations of the 40 years of the DDR turned into an unexpected happy ending. Some 500,000 people gathered in Berlin's Alexanderplatz on September 4, 1989, beginning the huge human rights movement which was to see the final act, the collapse of the DDR as an entity, within a few months.

Hungary had already begun dismantling their iron curtain in August, 1989, and many East Germans were using the road through Budapest to reach Vienna and on to West Germany. The pivotal moment had arrived. The cries of the demonstrators are revealing. First it was "Wir wollen raus"—"We want to leave, we want freedom". But secondly, beginning to realise their strength,

"Wir bleiben hier"—"We're staying here!" This was soon followed by "Wir sind das Volk" -"We are the people". (Not those "representatives" or puppet leaders who had for so long told everyone what to think.) And finally "Wir sind ein Volk"—"We are one people"—unity!

From the foundation of the DDR on October 7, 1949, past the tears of all the teachers and leaders of the nations of the East block when Stalin, the 'world genius' died in March, 1953, past the anti-fascist ramparts of 1961, past the hate and fear of the Cold War, to September, 1989, came a mighty push for freedom. Then Stalin's communist empire, which sprang like an ugly phoenix from the ashes of the Second World War and the territories liberated by the Soviet army, cracked and crumbled to dust. Countrywide the Stasi, part of 1.2 million East Germans under arms, had been preparing for a blood bath and to arrest huge numbers—in God' s goodness their preparations were never needed.

Since then, with free elections in every country, and with reunification in Germany in October 1990, there has been a transformation wrought all over Eastern Europe, nowhere more spectacularly than in East Germany. The Stasi-culture, fear, repression and illiberalism of 40 years has disappeared, but so has the certainty of employment, of cheap housing, of child-care provisions, healthcare and familiar networks of people and issues. Life in the new Central Europe opens opportunities, choices, and mobility for some, but spells poverty, exclusion, resignation and fear for others.

The gems of East German industry, though fatally flawed, glowed in the crown of the Soviet Empire. Now they have turned into places of misery and desolation. In Bitterfeld, an industrial chemical and power generating town between Berlin and Leipzig, those industries, founded over 125 years ago, were held up by Honecker's regime as a triumph of the urban proletariat. In reality they turned out to be filthy, unsafe and unproductive. Bitterfeld's only accolade was to be declared the most polluted spot in the world. It's air was yellow-green while its chimneys belched 120,000 tonnes of sulphur dioxide every year.

Now much of the old industry is defunct. Despite billions

of deutschmarks in aid from the federal government, most of those who worked in the factories are unemployed. The few West German and foreign firms, such as BASF, Bayer, and the Akzo Nobel Chemical company from Sweden which have invested make sure their operations are capital intensive. Many West German companies bought East German factories only to close them down when they proved unprofitable. Others invest across the border in the Czech Republic or in Poland where labour costs are lower.

Bitterfeld's only claim to fame now is its poverty. 30% of the population is unemployed, including 52% of the women. It takes months of hunting for even well qualified people to find jobs. Many will never work again. Most managers in the surviving factories are from West Germany. The local people show no sign of being able or willing to reshape their lives. Instead of starting new enterprises they sit back, survive on state handouts and grow angry and bitter. Ugly nationalism has been flourishing. Few think of moving to another part of Germany—West Germany is an alien culture.

Starting a new business in East Germany is difficult. Credit is hard to come by and a deep rooted dependency culture stems from 65 years of authoritarian rule, first by the Nazis and then by the Communists. There is no culture to support small start-up firms, take risks or spot winners. The handout culture has been in full swing since reunification. First valuable deutschmarks were exchanged for worthless East German marks, then wave after wave of Chancellor Kohl's West-East subsidies were topped up by local support.

Across the border in Poland, just a couple of hundred kilometres away in Wrocław by stark relief there is more motivation, more 'arbeitslust' than East German apathy. Wrocław is booming. Unemployment is down to eight per cent, growth is more than 10 per cent and thousands of new enterprises start each year. Many also fail, but the balance is positive. The streets are filled with smartly dressed shoppers and with new shops offering all manner of new services, computer training, flower delivery, popping up every week.

Yet Wrocław, pre 1945 the German city of Breslau, suffers

many of the same disadvantages endured by its German cousin Bitterfeld. Decades of communist rule, outrageously priced credit (loans at 30% per year, inflation at 11%) and an eroded industrial base. Wrocław has had no help to pull itself up by its bootstraps, no billions from Bonn, and Poland is isolated with a much weaker infrastructure than Germany and is much poorer: the average wage is less than half that in Bitterfeld and the cost of living almost as high. The old and the unemployed suffer as they never do in Germany.

Yet Wrocław appears rich, thriving. There are around 60,000 small companies in and around Wrocław. The mood is very positive. "If you don't have a job in Wrocław, you create your own, and if it fails you create another." In theory it should be easier to succeed in Germany. It can take months for a new business to install a single telephone, but Poles jump to mobile phones. People in Wrocław are fond of saying they started again once and they can do so again. Virtually all of the city's population was displaced from what is now the Ukraine after the end of the Second World War. But the Poles are filled with enthusiasm. They have suffered for most of their history, so they don't pin their hopes on others.

By contrast, the Germans in Bitterfeld, come from a race that has historically been in charge, and from a culture in which they are used to obeying orders. East Germany had a command economy before, during and after Communism. For Poland, Communism was an unfortunate interruption. Their spirit of enterprise never died. Many young people strive to learn English, as it will help them in any walk of life, so the Language School, started by Ruth Kowalczuk in 1989 at the Baptist church in Wrocław is brimming with hundreds of young students. Through committed Christian teachers and Christian holidays together many of the students have come to faith alongside gaining an excellent knowledge of English.

Yet even in East Germany the picture is not entirely bleak. What happened to Christian students in the German Democratic Republic under their fierce communist rulers? Did they survive the pressures? How did they cope with Marxist materialism? Hartmut Zopf became staff worker in the Student Mission in the GDR in 1975. This work was no offshoot or plant from the West—it arose under God "spontaneously" due to perceived need, and still meets the needs of students under today's vastly changed circumstances.

How did it happen? Hartmut was not yet a student when he was inspired by Dr. Klaus Richter. In Hartmut's own words he told me:-

"Dr. Richter saw the urgent need of helping students coming from a Christian background to hold on to their faith and not to fall away. Many of them had lost touch with the church. He saw this time and again, and many students also said that something should be done to prevent this happening. This falling away was being caused partly by liberal theology, and also by the overall atmosphere in the universities. There was no unequivocal, biblically faithful witness at the universities. All there was were the so called "student congregations" of the established Churches (Catholic and Lutheran). Now these did not have the same objective. The objective should have been that the Bible should be central and the students' questions regarding faith should be properly answered. The other great objective was to bring unbelieving students to Christ.

"I was due to start my university studies at the Karl Marx university in Leipzig in 1968, the exact date being 21st August, 1968. This was the day when the Russian troops invaded Czechoslovakia.

"I did not arrive at the university from home, I hadn't been listening to the news and had no idea what had happened.

"All the prospective students were gathered in the great aula or assembly hall of the university in Leipzig, and the very first thing we were told was that on this very day the friendly armies (of the Warsaw Pact) had marched into Czechoslovakia. (Because they thought communism was in danger of coming to an end through Dubček's "Prague Spring".)

"Then came all the entrance formalities, all the would-be students of theology were duly registered, except me. So I asked, "What about me?"

"Your papers are not here, sir", I was told.

So I asked, "Where are they then?"

"Well, if they are not here, they will be in your home town," I was told, "in the possession of the local military authorities."

"Be that as it may, my papers were not there, so I had to return home. However, I had already indicated my intent not to do active military service because I did not want to use weapons. Since 1964 there had been the possibility of refusing to do active military service in the German Democratic Republic for reasons of conscience and faith (i.e. to be a conscientious objector.) People who chose to do this had to take part in the construction of military installations, but they did not have to shoot. The GDR was the only country within the whole of Eastern Europe where you could do this without being imprisoned.

"So I went back home to my local army command and enquired when I would have to go to the army. "In May, 1969. Until then you can continue with your civil work", I was told.

"At that time I was working at a railway depot. I was called up again in April, 1969, but I was told that I would not be called up in May after all, and that in September I could start my studies at the university. This turned out to be what actually happened. Humanly speaking I lost a year but, from a spiritual point of view, I believe I gained a year as, during this time of waiting, God prepared me for my studies.

"We had to study Marxism/Leninism, having three sessions per week—two of them being lectures and one a time of discussion. After four years of study (eight semesters, each of them being half an academic year) we had to sit a state examination in this subject.

"In the first year we had historical materialism, in the second political economy, and in the third scientific socialism. In the fourth year we had a collection of everything.

"However, we had a much bigger problem than Marxism, and that was liberal theology. And for our Church (the state Church or Lutheran Church) this combination of a communist state and liberal theology was a deadly mix.

"And now let me come back to Dr. Richter. He did three things:-

"Firstly, he invited us for a special summer retreat for students. These retreats took place in a house at Wolkersdorf just outside Berlin. They were a great blessing for the students who took part. We would spend about 10 days together. The very first retreat at which I was present was led by Pastor Uwe Holmer[5], who later, after 1989, took Erich Honecker into his home. Pastor Holmer gave the Bible lectures. At this time he was the principal of the Bible school at Falkenberg near Berlin. During this retreat several of the students came to faith in Christ. These students then returned to their youth groups inspired to work for the Lord. The following year these students invited their friends so gradually the number of participants increased from 40 in 1968 to 70 in 1972.

"At this time we had no contact whatsoever with IFES. Your visit to us in 1975 was the very first contact possible.

"In the 1970's there were no actual, formal student groups. The very first group made up purely of students came into existence in Karl-Marx-Stadt, and that was before we had any contact with IFES.

"At the retreat in 1972 we were, once again, very conscious of God's work among us. After the evening sessions more and more students would go and talk to the pastor who was leading this retreat, because they had realised that, without Christ, they were lost. I believe there were something like 20 to 30—at any rate, many students came to faith. Students were queuing up late into the night to have counselling.

"During these retreats we were often conscious of a spiritual battle going on, as some of those present had some involvement with the occult. I remember one particular retreat where some of the students had formed an outright opposition group, openly resisting the message about the cross. But then God spoke to one after the other and they were all converted apart from one.

"Dr. Richter's second contribution was to invite students of theology to weekend seminars. These took place twice a year and they were intended to help theological students to survive spiritually during their time at university.

"Thirdly, Dr. Richter encouraged us to organise small group meetings with other Christian students in our towns, particularly

so as to be able to pray together. Whenever he was free, he would travel all over the GDR to visit these groups and take part in these prayer meetings himself.

"Towards the end of my studies I was asked by those responsible for this student work if I could imagine myself as the first staff worker. Up until then (1974) there had only been voluntary staff doing this work. I was then invited to do it from 1st January, 1975. Since 1990 this work has been united in East and West Germany on an all-German basis under the name of Studentenmission in Deutschland (SMD), i.e. the "Eastern" and the "Western" branches of the mission have united."

Chua Wee Hian was also impressed by Uwe Holmer, and wrote about it in his book "Getting Through Customs" [6] in the chapter titled 'Amazing Love'.

"I shall never forget my first visit to East Germany in November, 1981. After weeks of waiting I received a diplomatic visa and was considered an honoured guest of the State and Church. My bags were not even checked when I presented them for customs clearance.

My first assignment was to speak at the student conference at Falkenberg. There I met Pastor Uwe Holmer, who was the director of the Bible school. The Holmers had ten children. I learnt that the older ones could not get into university because they had publicly professed the Christian faith and at the same time refused to join the Young Marxist League. This meant that they had to compete for the tiny quota of places reserved for non-Marxists.

A month after my visit to East Germany, our family was over the moon when Andrew (our son) was accepted as a scholar at Pembroke College, Oxford. After the euphoria I remembered Pastor Holmer and his children in East Germany and thought to myself, 'How would I have reacted if Andrew were rejected by his university simply because he was a committed Christian? How would I have advised him?' For us it was only a hypothetical situation, but for the Holmers, it was a grim reality.

In the autumn of 1989 East Germany was all over the papers and on our TV screens. The citizens of East Germany had marched against their government demanding freedom and reunification with West Germany. Soon the much feared and hated president, Erich Honecker, was discredited. Amidst the social and political convulsions Pastor Holmer's name shot into prominence. I had almost forgotten him and it took me some time to recall that he was the same person that I had met in Falkenberg eight years previously. He had become the director of a Christian orphanage and of an old people's home. Pastor Holmer and his wife personally invited the Honeckers to stay in their family home. No other East German family would have extended their welcome to this infamous couple.

Mrs Honecker was the former Minister of Education. She initiated the policy giving special preference to young Marxists to study at university. She was therefore indirectly responsible for discriminating against the Holmer children. Yet the Holmers responded so differently. They could, together with their countrymen, have poured scorn and contempt on the disgraced ex-president and his wife. Instead, they opened their home and hearts to their 'enemies'.

Would I have done that? Not likely! I was simply dumbfounded by the actions of the Holmers. With tears in my eyes, I prayed, 'Lord, thank you for this demonstration of your amazing love.'"

Some say that the churches were brave under communism, others that they were compromising, and filled with traitors. As foreigners, it is too easy to idealise, in either direction, what we do not know much about. Our own realities are better known. Yet the fact remains that whole nations need reconciliation, not only individuals who, under serious pressure or being misguided, denied their Lord.

LAYING THE FOUNDATIONS

Stacey would not have known or even dreamt of such historical developments as I outlined in the previous chapter, but his vision was there—unshakeable. He felt the pressures of the world always bearing in on people, and students were especially vulnerable to sin. But, if they were open to being led astray, they were also open to the call of the Lord Jesus, and when they had responded they were eager to win their peers.

Stacey Woods writing in "The Growth of a Work of God"[7] quotes Charles Troutman "who, in the early days of the movement, coined the expression 'continuing kindergarten' to describe the student university community. These two words aptly describe the primary and essential spiritual problem facing a student movement. It may have strong tradition, a stated purpose and doctrinal platform, but in a sense it has no permanent foundation or roots. A student worker is like a person standing beside a slowly flowing, broad river. He looks upstream, water is approaching him, now it is moving in front of him, now it has passed him forever. Always there is a flow of students into the university and four (or three or five) years later, all too soon, a flow out..."

The focus of the IFES was strongly on student initiative, but a staff member could come alongside, rather like an elder brother, to spark an interest, inspire, or coach. And, like the best headmaster, Stacey had found men and women of breadth and wisdom, vision and maturity to share this work with him. They were people, I found, who enjoyed life in all its richness and fullness in every facet that the good Lord had made. The range of their outside interests and abilities enriched my own life, astounded me then and cheers me now. As fellow Christians we worked together in almost flawless harmony, whether from Brethren, Baptist, Methodist, Lutheran, Reformed or Anglican Churches. Divisions which normally separate Christian people into their denominations hardly worried us and never seemed to show. We accepted each other's sincerity to sink our trivial differences and to work together for our great goal, for our great God.

Among these lovely people who Stacey had chosen to be our fellow staff members my wife and I made friends whom we have cherished throughout our life. Students themselves were and are the true strength of student work. That work was and is the winning of students by students for Christ, and building them up to serve God in their professions and in the leadership of their countries. But they needed a few staff, like the catalyst in a chemical reaction, to inspire the troops, encourage them when they were having a hard time, and even to go and find Christian students. Then staff could gather them together to study God's Word and teach them how to win their friends to Christ. Without those few staff nothing would have happened in the way it did! We did not often, if ever, meet with staff of other similar organisations, yet I soon became convinced that our fellow staff members in IFES had been as truly called of God and equipped by him to do this special task as we had. They were almost always inspired, well motivated and giving of their best, so that under God, they'd be a jolly hard team to beat!

Stacey Woods had the desire to find staff who were truly called by God, not volunteers, who he said he often found profoundly unsatisfactory. "Those led by the Holy Spirit who were invited to become staff workers generally made their mark, some going on to larger ministries. Strangely many of the volunteers proved to be 'also rans', "and some flopped badly," he wrote.[8]

I certainly found Stacey Woods a great boss to work for, an inspiring, liberating General Secretary. Other staff would probably agree with me, by and large. Occasionally Stacey could be abrasive or touchy. He was a fallen human being too. "What we were, what we were becoming in Christ," wrote Stacey, "was infinitely more important than any activity because we believed that the quality and worth of all that we did from an eternal perspective depended on the kind of persons we really were in our inner selves. God's essential method is men and women, not technique."[9]

After leaving Poland in 1968 I worked for a while at Redhill, England in a chemical research laboratory. There was a very bad atmosphere among the staff, and I soon learned how demoralising it is not to have enough work to do. There were routine tests to run, observations to record at regular intervals. I weighed, measured, observed and wrote reports. In truth it was incredibly boring. There was no inspiration, no vision of where that company was going and what we were trying to achieve. What a contrast to working under Stacey Woods! I realised how much happier people are when they are under a bit of pressure, feeling they are being stretched to give of their best, rather than when they are trying to fill the time, trying to concentrate hour after hour on instrument panels, dials or scales. It was just as though, as with David in Psalm 78:71, "God took me from tending the sheep to be the shepherd of his people."

Stacey shared his great vision of the wide overall situation and insights gleaned from his travels to encourage staff in many parts of the world. I found this intensely inspiring and motivating. He was always happy to make time to sit down and discuss our situation, progress or problems. Never did we fail to pray together or find that God had no way forward. Stacey oversaw the pioneering work throughout the world. The function of IFES is to co-ordinate existing member movements such as Inter-Varsity, usually one in each country, and extend the work in countries where there is as yet no formally organised work. Stacey's field was dispersed to such an extent that we were mostly left to organise our own sections of the show and get on with the job ourselves. I was given an almost totally free hand. Stacey could not exercise any real day-to-day control. We were mostly on one year contracts. If you did not seem to be making the grade, or slacked off, or ran out of steam, there was no guarantee you would still have a job!

Stacey had a vision which was simple, stretching and an inspiration for all the staff. So we were always striving to improve some aspect of our activities. It was quality rather than quantity. "Never despise the day of small things," was a motto he often repeated. Yet his vision encompassed high spiritual values as well as achievements. I am certain that this wide vision was the best gift God gave to Stacey Woods. Without it decentralisation, trust, tolerance and the setting of aims for each member of staff would have been impossible. With it we had the most potent team-building weapon. We all worked willingly together, shoulder to shoulder, because we knew where we were going! It was Stacey's vision that kept us on our toes, humanly speaking, though we all felt our higher and more important motivation was to serve God to the very best of our ability. From this came our willingness to take initiatives, and in turn let the students take theirs. The IFES was our resource, our means, rather than our master.

The work was hard, often to the point of exhaustion, but very rewarding, and almost always enormous fun. Well over a hundred million people live in the countries located between Germany and Russia. From January, 1970, we toured throughout Eastern Europe, visiting the students we found out about from church leaders and encouraging them to serve Christ their Lord where they were. Students can, and should, be called to Christian service. As Stacey writes in "Growth of a Work of God" we "present the call of God to the foreign missions field and so help all students discover God's role for them, at home or abroad, in worldwide evangelization." At that time, with severe restrictions on travel, the possibilities for serving the Lord were naturally confined more to service in their home situations. The main help we could offer them in this was through our international summer vacation Bible courses, giving in-depth training which would send students back home thrilled with the Bible and eager to work with fresh zeal for their Lord. This was the hub of Stacey's strategy, investment in people.

The courses aimed essentially to expand the students' minds

on the teaching of one or two books of the Bible, and to give them guidelines on personal evangelism and on the use of the small Bible study group as an evangelistic tool. Few students seemed able to articulate their faith, and many were intimidated by the world they found at university. They were often zealous, but still needed to grow in their faith. Often students could be quite dogmatic on ethical issues, but with little ability to reason a firmly held position. There was a great need to train them to be confident in the gospel. Even students from the most robust of the evangelical churches could have rather low levels of biblical understanding. Bible seminaries being under severe pressure, very few theological books were available, and student numbers in them were strictly limited. So pastors were not particularly well taught anywhere in Eastern Europe. Anyway, their sermons would inevitably be geared to the average church member rather than to the university student. We needed to give guidance on very practical matters such as how to make students' friends feel at home and how to address their real problems while studying the Bible together, so that they would meet the risen Lord Jesus Christ, see his solution to their needs and want to go on following him in every area of their lives. On these ten-day to two-week courses we could spend more useful study periods with student leaders than over many years of "normal" visiting at home or in study situations.

We also had time to listen to the students, learn to understand and appreciate their real needs, pray with them as well as to get the students to begin to pray and work together. This was always by far the best situation, where real co-operation developed, and where students would go home from a course ready to encourage one another, and to sharpen each other. Stacey Woods was keen to teach students to pray together. "Prayer", he wrote,[10] "spells all the difference between working for God in our own strength and wisdom or being fellow labourers together with him in the work that he is seeking to do in the university."

Stacey had the same vision for international work as he had had for the work in Canada and then the U.S. He writes,[11] "Inter-Varsity starts with an elementary but essential emphasis on the quiet time, prayer, learning to study the Scriptures, learning the gospel, the gift of God's grace but also its demands, and how to pass it on to others. We see students mature as Christians and as leaders, but by then it is the spring quarter of their final year. Sometimes we feel like mice on a rotating treadmill, teaching the same primary things continuously. We constantly strive but never arrive." This is true of the short term, but this book well illustrates how much Christian students have achieved in the long run, as they later became brave Christian leaders in many walks of life and in many difficult situations.

Stressing the importance of university days for making life's greatest decisions, Stacey added "Life shows us that if students leave the university without God, in the majority of cases they will continue to live the rest of their lives without him and to die without him." What an awesome responsibility for us who minister to and encourage students at a most vital and strategic time of their lives.

Groups do not always work well together as if by some natural law. They need help to grow and enable each person to develop a unique role and contribution, so that collectively they are able to go out to achieve their goals. Jesus brought his disciples together with him, before he sent them out, two by two. Anikó and I were also a team of two. While assisting the students individually, counselling, befriending and challenging them, and trying to ensure all our discussions together were meaningful, we especially wanted them to form working friendships with other students. As a staff member I could invite students from different churches to our conferences. People who would never meet 'at home' in their own countries, who could even be members of different congregations in the same town, came to discover each other and learn that they shared the same vision. The effect was electric.

The venue for many of our Bible courses was the delightful and romantic Schloss Mittersill, a castle not far from Salzburg in Austria which Stacey had recently had transformed into a student conference centre. Under staff coaching we saw little groups forming at Mittersill which functioned perfectly 'back home' in the different countries. The credit for what they achieved should go to them. It is the chemicals which react together to form an exciting new product, but the conditions for the reaction, temperature and pressure, often have to be just right. The catalyst stays behind when the reaction has been completed, but it also needs to be there! As catalysts we had to make sure people could develop their vital gifts—the job called for skill, study, practice and example. It was almost always immense fun.

In fact I believe a leavening of humour needs to prevail, almost be a way of life, and the more so under the tough conditions we were experiencing in Eastern Europe at the time. I shall always remember a friend sitting and studying in the next room while, with a small group of friends, I shared in a Bible study. My friend who was quietly studying was amazed—our group was almost dying with laughter (unfortunately I do not recall which passage of the Bible we were studying at the time). He could hardly believe we were studying the Bible. But if you think you need a long face and a dour expression to be a real Christian or to share your faith—relax! It is usually better to have a sense of fun. Jesus certainly did. Despite first century Jewish jokes being far removed from our own cultural conventions his teaching includes the entertaining metaphors of a plank of wood sticking out of our own eye and a camel passing through the eye of a needle!

The staff had to be prepared for all types of work when it came to putting on the conferences—even what seemed to us something very much like dancing, when Hans Bürki led us all in 'rhythmic exercises' done to music outside in the courtyard during one Mittersill conference. Help might also be needed in cooking the meals. During the time we spent in Austria preparing invitations for the East European students I became rather good at roasting a single chicken in the huge castle ovens designed to feed over a hundred people! Likewise I recall spending my time during one very international and grand 'Quadrennial General Committee' operating the washing-up machine and drying the cutlery. But it was well worth being there for the inspiring meetings and mutual help, from as far away as New Zealand, which flowed to Eastern Europe afterwards.

One evening before we started a conference I was sewing the pages of the conference song book together. It was hot off the press, (an old fashioned spirit duplicator, to be more accurate). I was collating and then sewing the sheets with the large stitches our ancient sewing machine could produce, when Ada Lum, a gifted colleague who had collected and typed the songs (as well as being the noble soul who turned the handle on the duplicator), introduced me to the General Secretary of Canadian Inter-Varsity who, to my embarrassment, had just happened to drop by. Tall and genial Tony Tyndale, who left England to become a staff worker in the Canadian movement after Stacey Woods had set up Inter-Varsity there, didn't blink an eye. He must have been accustomed, himself, to doing lots of mundane and less glamorous jobs than his title would suggest.

If you ever go in for missionary work, you'll probably also need to develop a large amount of tolerance for the lack of systems which would drive people in more profitable parts of the world's economy round the bend with frustration and annoyance. Everything and everyone needs to be accepted as a gift from God, or as an opportunity to be grasped and turned around for him! Even if everything that can go wrong seems to be going wrong, it is not by malice or design. It may be because of the almost unbelievable absurdity of the communist system, or any Third World government's system, or because of lack of funds or people to do the work, but it is always an opportunity to prove God's grace. Personally I always found scope for endless initiative and fun.

The pay was not great, but the reward of seeing God at work in the lives of students in university towns all over Eastern Europe was very satisfying in itself. And if the pay would not stretch to us having expensive holidays we were often in different places, which was itself very refreshing in comparison with the daily grind between home and office or factory which is the lot of much of the world's population.

We worked together as a staff team and, over time, saw the tremendously increased effectiveness of the freely-given collaboration of a splendid group of men and women of God. At Mittersill we had the time needed for this to happen naturally. It is in an ideally spacious and relaxing setting among woods and meadows and up in the hills two kilometres away from the bustle of the village. The effort to make it happen was small in comparison with the dividends it brought.

We did enjoy the occasional unexpected bonus. I vividly recall the time when in October, 1970, Hans Bürki, whose wife is also Hungarian, invited us to spend a week in his delightful modernised vine planter's shack. He told us that he often took a break there himself when he returned from a long journey away from home visiting students. After recovering from the exhaustion of travel he would invite his wife to join him.

In this way Hans taught by action and example. The shack stands on a hill in northern Switzerland with a splendid view over a quiet valley. The vines were all around, their leaves golden in the autumn and rustling in the breezes. Apart from that it was peace, perfect peace; Switzerland without a holidaymaker in sight. We could unwind, recover and explore. We felt richly privileged and blessed by this one special unexpected gift. What a rich reward, which we would never have had if we had not been working alongside Hans in IFES. There and then we determined that we too would make our cottage in Sussex, England, available to other staff. Several, including the family of Chua Wee Hian who followed Stacey Woods as IFES General Secretary and then

the family and friends of Brede Kristensen who was European Regional Secretary of IFES and later Hans Bürki did appreciate, during successive summers, our slightly different but also very personal gift of hospitality.

I had known Hans since my first contact with IFES when during my last long student vacation I had attended a six-week-long 'formation' training course which Hans led at Casa Moscia and at Rasa in the Ticino region in southern Switzerland.

Casa Moscia is a rambling collection of buildings on Lake Maggiore adapted for parties of students. It belongs to the German speaking Swiss IFES movement. Lemons grow outside in many of the gardens along the lake, such is the mild, wonderful winter climate that it virtually never freezes! But the mountains bring down the rain—and tiny streams become raging torrents in an hour or two when it starts to rain. Between storms we swam in the lake, and then one day took a bus and cable car swinging out across a ravine-like valley up to Rasa, not far as the crow flies, but high above Locarno and the lakeside Moscia and almost as far removed in time as well with its heavy grey stone dwellings. It was a special time for me—six weeks is enough time to get to know people really well, to have a disagreement and to build the relationship really strong again afterwards. I always felt particularly close to Hans Bürki after this initial Bible and Life course he led. When later he visited us I remember Hans removing his shoes and walking barefoot around one of our great Sussex gardens, just enjoying the feel of nature as God had made it as well as its sights and sounds. In Switzerland too he taught us through lectures and assignments but also by attitude and by doing things together. He took us away for some days to Rasa, that primitive remote village high in the mountains, where we could be away from civilisation and close to God. Later he had us all take boats out on the lake in the evening after dark, sing to God in our different languages and share some experiences of our lives as we had tried to live them for God.

9 GUESTS AND GRADUATES

Toward the end of the 1960s Stacey Woods had a vision for a place in the middle of Europe where students could meet. He was burdened particularly for Christian students from the poorer countries of Southern and Eastern (largely Catholic and Orthodox) Europe. The work in this area was still undeveloped largely owing to the rule of communism in Eastern Europe since the Second World War ended in 1945.

Bringing students together was important because in meeting each other they would suddenly discover that their own little corner of the globe is not so bad after all in comparison to someone else's patch! In meeting they would find fellowship and friendship despite all sorts of man-made, cultural, political, denominational and linguistic barriers. I recall Christian Israelis and Christian Arabs together at a student Bible course long before their political masters began to shake hands.

By the mid 1990's formal IFES international student conferences drawing hundreds or thousands of students were being held in Poland and in Hungary, but in the 1970's this would have been out of the question. The local KGB or secret police would never have allowed it. However, after the Helsinki accords of 1965, which 'guaranteed' certain human rights, some students could, often with considerable difficulty, travel out from East to Western Europe. We had tried using Casa Moscia, the home of the VBG (Vereinigte Bibelgruppen in Schule Universität Beruf), the German speaking Swiss student movement, which lies south of Locarno on Lake Maggiore, but it was a struggle to persuade Swiss families to invite students from Eastern Europe, as each student needed a personal invitation before they could stand any chance of being granted a passport or a Swiss visa. Then they really did have to go to their host families in case they were quizzed about their visit by the secret police on their return home.

Then again there was the cost of travel to Switzerland. It was much higher than to Austria and Eastern Europeans had no convertible currency to buy their own tickets in Western Europe. All needed tickets to be bought and sent to them, and pocket money given to them when they arrived. Added to which, Switzerland was probably the most expensive country in Western Europe. Eastern European students arriving in Switzerland were agog at the sumptuous shop window displays, the high fashions and the huge expense of everything!

At this point Stacey Woods heard about a pale pink castle at Mittersill, not far from Salzburg in the middle of Austria, built around 1150 A.D., which was now almost abandoned. In recent years Schloß Mittersill had been a hunting lodge for the rich and famous. Queen Juliana of the Netherlands and Prince Bernhardt spent their honeymoon there, and the Shah of Persia slept well there before Iran turned into a powder keg which deposed the Shah and turned itself into an Islamic state. For 600 years before that, this castle had been a residence of the Prince Archbishop of Salzburg.

Stacey was not just a starry-eyed idealist. He lived in the real world and knew he would need a great deal of help to buy and fix up this castle as a student centre. However, he had very fine friends back in the USA. Soon, with a group of them, who formed IFES, Inc., Stacey bought and refurbished Schloß Mittersill, two kilometres up the hill to the north of the village of Mittersill and with the simple but usefully anonymous address of Thalbach 1.

Schloss Mittersill

Stacey shared his view of the need and the opportunity. "Coincident with the move of the IFES office to Switzerland, was the burden and vision of reaching students in the Eastern European communist block for Christ. It was obvious that a training centre and refuge for these students was needed, and Austria, whose neutrality was recognized both by West and East, seemed to be an obvious choice for such a centre.[12]

"It was an answer to prayer quietly waiting upon God that John Bolten Jr. of Nürnberg, who knew of this burden and was a member of the Schloß Mittersill Club, got in touch with me telling me that the Schloß was up for sale. I shall never forget the morning that he and I met Baron Hubert von Pantz at Kitzbühel and motored to Mittersill. Immediately the possibilities of this place seized us.

"But there were two seemingly insurmountable hurdles. The first was the asking price, $600,000, which was to include 80% of the furnishings; the second was the attitude of the IFES committee which was adamantly opposed to owning property and the feeling that to have such a centre in Europe would create an invidious distinction in relation to Africa, Latin America and the Far East.

"It would seem that Mittersill was God's gift to the movement. In spite of these oppositions, the castle was eventually purchased

for $100,000, and a reluctant consent was wrung from the IFES committee on the definite understanding that the IFES would never be asked to own the property. So in a sense Mittersill has been an IFES orphan, perhaps for some almost a bone in the throat of the IFES. It was owned by the purchasing body, IFES Inc.[13] *(an independent body in the U.S. existing to further IFES International in the United States) which assumed all responsibility and raised money both for the purchase and necessary improvements, backed by the U.S. Inter-Varsity.*

"God has greatly used Mittersill...None of this was accomplished without struggle, agonizing prayer, misunderstanding and great difficulty, but, thank God, Mittersill continues as a centre of God's work not only in reaching students in Eastern Europe but in strengthening and training leaders from around the world."

Students could arrive by bus or on the quaint narrow gauge railway from Zell-am-See. The train winds its way along the floor of the Pinzgau valley keeping company with the Salzach stream (a sizeable river by the time it reaches Salzburg). The castle is just sufficiently remote for students, especially those from Eastern Europe, not to rush off to the bright lights of any town or to be tempted on shopping sprees for things they had never seen in the shops back home. With its excellent library it greatly encourages a peaceful air of study, but is not too remote. Even an occasional bus comes past the gate as it descends over Paß Thurn from Kitzbühel. Then again, the standard of living in Austria, while Western, is hardly as extravagant or expensive as in Switzerland which makes it more conducive to a happy stay and return home. Stacey was not aiming to help students to flee and claim political asylum, not that there were ever many of those. His vision was to help and inspire them in their spiritual lives so that they could return to strengthen the churches in the East.

Stacey himself describes one main goal in his book "Growth of a Work of God" page 95. "We believed—and still do—that the key to personal spiritual development is first of all a daily period for a real meeting with the living God through the Holy Spirit and the Scriptures. So at all camps, conferences and training sessions, time was set aside usually before breakfast for such a "divine-human encounter." This became a top priority...

"At student conferences, training was given to students in order to help them to have a more effective quiet time. Discussion groups would be held following the quiet time in order to assist one another to discover how best and how meaningfully such a time could be spent. This regulated practice in camps, conferences and training sessions was but an attempt to help students to establish such a habit in personal daily life."

It was one of our primary tasks to find the crucial Christian leaders among the students, those who would benefit from international exposure, from good Bible teaching, from training in evangelism and in how to write and lead Bible studies. Then they could return to witness to their friends, form little Bible study groups for mutual encouragement and for outreach among their fellow students. We aimed to bring those who eventually would be leaders in different walks of life in their societies. Strategically as it turned out, though we did not realise it at the time, they also became national workers of the emerging student movements in their different countries when political tensions between East and West eased, the Iron Curtain fell, and the Berlin Wall came down.

Did Stacey's pink castle with its breathtaking views over the Pinzgau valley to the High Tauern mountains, make it seem to the students from economically hard pressed Eastern and Southern Europe that IFES shared a certain amount of heaven's power and glory? There were spacious grounds where we walked and played. When over 100 came the overflow was housed in the Neidhaüsel, the little house close by where local prisoners used to be kept till the Prince Archbishop of Salzburg came round to hold his court and condemn at least some of them to the castle's dungeons.

Perhaps the castle experience was a treat for our students. We tried to make it a spiritual treat, and if the weather was kind, which it was not guaranteed to be among the mountains, it was often a marvellous treat all round. National camps in Eastern Europe were typically held under canvas in fields or in barns on farms, and certainly in much less salubrious surroundings. But as IFES depends on front line troops, (unpaid student volunteers), for over 99% of its work, it always brought rich dividends to gently coax, cajole and treat them cordially at Mittersill. It helped them to share your vision and work together rather than against you.

Chua Wee Hian met a little 'culture clash' at Mittersill. He writes,[14] *"Alcoholic drinks can stir up bitter controversy. At an international conference (at Mittersill) in Austria the leadership team sought my advice. African Christians were horrified that the conference centre sold beer and served wine to certain guests. They thought it was most unchristian to serve the demon spirit of alcohol and wanted the leaders to ban it. They declared dogmatically that it was the wrong spirit for an international Christian conference.*

At the same conference our team received written suggestions from the Spanish delegation; they were very disappointed because table wine was not served with the midday and evening meals. They urged that the situation be rectified as soon as possible.

It would have been tempting to study the Scriptures on wine. There are verses which describe wine making glad the heart of man (Psalm 104:15). Jesus' first miracle was to turn six huge jars of water into wine (John 2—NIV suggests between 450 to 690 litres of vintage wine). Paul urged Timothy to take some wine for his stomach (1 Timothy 5:23). I'm always fascinated by anti-wine Christians, insisting that this wine was no more than unfermented grape juice. In the case of Timothy, one resourceful commentator remarked that the wine was 'not for internal consumption but for external application'.

Equally, the Scriptures do warn against drunkenness and excessive imbibing of strong drinks (see Isaiah 5:11,12 and Ephesians 5:18) and causing our brothers to stumble by what we eat or drink (Romans 14:20,21).

In the end I suggested that African Christians and the Spanish folk should have an informal Bible study on Romans 14. That proved to be a wonderful solution to their debate.'"

Erna Kull, a Swiss, told me how, soon after she started as

a secretary in the IFES Lausanne office in 1968, Stacey Woods asked her to translate into German a brochure about the first student conference in Mittersill. She was not sure about some technical expressions, and phoned Hans Bürki to enquire about the correct usage. Stacey overheard the conversation, and began to expostulate about Erna running up the phone bill.

"He started jumping up and down shouting at me to put the phone down," said Erna. Hans could hear this going on down the line. "What's the old shouter going on about now?" said Hans, comforting Erna! On other occasions the situation was reversed, with Stacey soothing Erna over difficult conversations with Hans! As in every walk of life, prickly individuals do exist, but the only way forward in God's kingdom is to walk in the light God gives, being open and honest with one another. This generally does produce a more understanding response. That is the way we can build one another up, and help one another go forward with the Lord.

In 1969 Erna was Stacey's German interpreter at Mittersill while Anikó was interpreting for Viktor Sudár, the first Hungarian ever to be there for a Bible course. Earlier, in the Lausanne office, Erna had prepared the invitation letters for Viktor, and prayed that he might receive his passport and be allowed to travel. She was overjoyed to be in Mittersill and to see how God had answered her prayers, never dreaming that this tall young medical student would eventually become her husband!

Stacey's wife, Yvonne writes very movingly of the first year that Schloß Mittersill was up and running, 1968.

"There was everything to discourage, and many to voice the problems: heating in winter, expenses, transportation of students, securing help to run a castle!...But God raised up helpers and funds and sent students. There were 20 in that first summer from Czechoslovakia. They lapped up the teaching and spent their free time copying by hand page after page of English Bible commentaries, later to be translated into their own language at home. They all arrived safely back home just hours before the August invasion

of communist troops! The door to return was then closed for the next 20 years. The castle continued to welcome students from many countries...In God's goodness a library was built up. A familiar sight day after day was young men and women seated in the library poring over the wealth of biblical commentaries. Only God knows the end from the beginning. From this centre the Lord has made his salvation known to the ends of the earth. Gatherings at the castle have truly been a foretaste of heaven with the fellowship of brothers and sisters from every continent, people and colour, of every nation—one in our Lord Jesus Christ." (Schloß Mittersill, 25th Anniversary)

What has happened to them? One of the Czechoslovak students who was able to travel to Mittersill a year later, in 1969, was Pavel Černý. I visited him, his wife Hanna and later their growing family, throughout my IFES days, to encourage him and take them helpful Christian literature. For a while he was based in a main street known as Revoluční in Kutná Hora, a very attractive and interesting mediaeval city some 50 miles east of Prague. (The street had been renamed after Masaryk, first president of Czechoslovakia, when I passed that way more recently, but there was no mention of Masaryk when the Communists were in power.) These visits were never by day, in case the neighbours noticed and informed the secret police. They were always in the evening with the car parked at a discreet distance. Now Pavel is the president of the Czech Brethren[15] based in Prague. When I visited Daniel Kaleta pastor of the Czech Brethren Church in Tábor in September 1995, he told me that Pavel Černý is a very gentle and loving man. A lifetime spent living under a difficult regime certainly leaves its mark, for good or for ill.

Pavel was somehow able to get into the ancient and famous Charles University in Prague in 1968, despite his family being known as Christians. At that time it was all but impossible for known Christians to be granted a place to study. He began by studying biology.

"When I got there, said Pavel, I saw different crises in people's

lives. It was very depressing to see people divorcing. I knew people who had tried to commit suicide after the Prague Spring was so severely put down by the Soviet troops in 1968. Many young people escaped from our country and a lot of people were very sad and depressed about the future. I wanted to help these people who were really in crisis, and I realised that my knowledge of the Bible was really very poor. So I decided to transfer to study theology.

"I was invited to Mittersill in 1969. It was really good to meet Christian leaders there who represented the evangelical movement, and I was also very much influenced by their lectures and the fellowship.

"It was really very special that, while Western Europe generally could seem to forget about us when the Soviet tanks rolled in to Prague, there were still Christian people coming over and trying to break that isolation. In 1969 it was still possible to get a passport, but after that for quite a number of years, it was almost impossible to get to the West.

"For me it was something like a miracle to be able to have fellowship with such a professor as Henri Blocher, people like René Padilla and Samuel Escobar, or just to listen to the lectures of Sir Fred Catherwood, who was a member of the European Parliament. Henri Blocher spent about an hour with me one afternoon explaining points, and being so patient with me, as my knowledge of French was not very good then. Just to see such people as professing Christians was very important for us, because in our country all people who were holding high positions were atheists, but at Mittersill it was possible to meet people working for the government and still professing Christians. I was still very uncertain about the future of my studies, and that conference helped me very much.

"At college, I remember some of my colleagues talking as though they were atheists, and it was very sad to see that. I think liberal theology tries to see problems everywhere. If there are none, it is necessary to develop some! The liberals are also prejudiced about some things, and it was very difficult to obtain a place to study theology as numbers were very limited by the State. During the time of the Communists the faculty of theology was not recognised as even part of the Charles University, so I received my degree

officially only after the Velvet Revolution. The Communists kept theologians away because they didn't want them to mix with other students and influence them.

"When I finished my studies, in 1974, my denomination had to ask for a special licence for me to preach. I was called in by the Secretary of State for Religious Affairs. He was very friendly to me and said: " Well, you are a young man but you should think about another job, because in five or ten years there will be no Church in our country." I didn't say it out loud, but I was thinking that there were others, like Nero, who had said that too. Now our Church is growing all over the country. We have appointed Daniel Fajfr as our national evangelist, and I am busy appointing new pastors, opening new church buildings and interviewing prospective candidates for the ministry."

Daniel Kaleta also had serious troubles with the authorities. Daniel is spry, compact and bright-eyed. His face and hands are as expressive as his speech. He is a raconteur, and the telling of his tale gave him pleasure. I had the impression, with him more than with others, that as he told it he was seeing the events he described afresh; that as he stared into the past the outcome was not yet obvious, and that when he looked at me, his clear eyes a touch hazy, he was still seeing the scenes he described, perhaps even hoping to understand them. Daniel is one of those Czechs who speak good Polish. We sat in a tiny room behind his church, a 1930's somewhat art deco building which nestles under tall trees close to an ancient gate in the mediaeval walled town of Tábor. Daniel explained to me:

"It was not easy to serve the Lord under the communist regime in Czechoslovakia—but it was always possible. I believe that at all times and in all places it is possible to serve the Lord. Even in the most difficult times those with a 'hot heart' found a way. In the 1950s many Czechoslovak pastors and church leaders were put in prison. There was a physical attack on the Church from the State. Many people were accused of something political and then imprisoned.

"When I began my ministry with my wife, Gražyna, it was not physical but psychological. Children could not get into high school if it was known that they were Christians. The state tried to frighten people. We often felt like Peter did when Jesus was on trial. "Aren't you one of his followers?" And Peter denied the Lord.

"At that time it was possible to be a Christian at home, but you were not supposed to talk openly about it. But there were always people who were brave. Dr Vlado Fajfr was a brave evangelist at this difficult time. He travelled around the churches and called people to follow Christ. I lived in a small village—Trhový Štěpánov. The church there had 50 to 60 members including some young people. Five of us formed a music group. We called it 'Cantri'. Dr. Vlado Fajfr invited us to sing at his evangelistic meeting. I well remember that Saturday evening: it was to be a special evening for young people. He called people to the front to indicate that they were willing to follow Christ and a few came. The other boys played, and I sang of how Jesus had died for us, how he gave his blood for us, and how we should come to him. I wanted other people to come to him, but then I began to realise that I hadn't come myself!

"Before the next service Dr Fajfr suggested that we should pray together for a fruitful meeting. During the prayers the Holy Spirit touched my heart and at that moment I realised that I was without God. I had been singing that God was Lord, but he wasn't Lord of my life. I sang that people should follow him, but I was still going my own way. I had always thought I was better than others, but now God showed me that I was also a sinner. I was proud and critical like the Pharisees in the Bible, and I was shocked when I saw my heart. At that moment I understood that I had to turn, not just in theory, but in practice, to come to Jesus and let him deal with me. I confessed and the Lord Jesus forgave me—peace and joy came into my heart. It happened so quietly—I told no one—the others there were praying but this was all going on in my heart. They did not know, but in the service I was a new person and I sang from my heart!

"In my life I thought I believed in God, but it had only been nominal. My father was a pastor, and I always said I was a Christian, but my heart had been my own. Later God showed me

that it wasn't enough to just change my heart, but I also had to be prepared to tell people that Jesus is my Lord—as it says in the Bible, to confess Christ before men. In life it was sometimes difficult to do this, because I knew I'd have trouble in school or in the army if I was known as a Christian. But Christ said that those who honour him, he will honour, and God always made a way for me, even with the help of non-Christian people, and it was always to God's glory. For example, it was supposedly impossible for me to get into any secondary or higher school because my father was a pastor, yet when I was 15 I was accepted into the grammar school! There in the grammar school there were a few Christians, and again we formed a music group and sang for the other students. We sang ordinary songs, and Christian songs too.

"When I was 17 a teacher came to me and said how much he liked our group, and that he'd organise a schools music festival. Others would sing and we could also contribute. It was held in a castle. There were hundreds of children there. We sang, but we had to sing the communist songs—nobody liked them. Then outside in the courtyard we played and sang our Christian songs. The response was overwhelming! After a few moments we seemed to have our own Christian festival. The children were pouring out to hear us. We sang and spoke briefly about Christ. There were always some opportunities like this. God closed the eyes or ears of those who could have been against us, and gave us such opportunities.

"Even in the army, where I was for two years on military service, and where it was not even possible to take a Bible, I had a whole Christian library to lend out to other national service conscripts as well as to the professional soldiers. Some people tried to close the library down, but God helped me.

"I'd been there for five months as a medical assistant and had had many opportunities to witness and to share my testimony. There were exams after these five months after which we would gain promotion and then take home leave. There were five exams, four about medicine and the fifth about politics. Before I went for that exam our teacher of politics told us to be very careful what we said. Why? I wondered. He was such a kind, older man. I was given two questions, and had 20 minutes to prepare my spoken answers.

The second question was 'How does the Church view the events of 1968?' (when there had been an attempt at a political counter revolution against the communists, and the Warsaw Pact forces, mainly the Soviet forces, came in to Czechoslovakia with 'Brotherly Help' to put it down).

"Here I was in front of the colonel who had especially given me this question because he knew me to be a Christian. Whatever I said could be wrong. But he allowed me 50 minutes, though normally only five minutes were allowed to give an answer. In 1968 I had only been 14 years old! I told him I was not responsible for the attitude of the Church in 1968, but I could not escape. He replied that I had been well-prepared politically, but that my mind was not right so I could not get a good mark to earn my promotion. "A young person does not have to kick," he said, "but to think straight." Then he told me that he would make sure I would not gain promotion or receive any privileges such as home leave. I had peace in my heart that I hadn't denied Christ. This colonel had supreme power over us in the army.

"The other conscripts asked why I had been so long. The one next to me in the queue for the exams had heard everything. He was a Christian too, but he said he was not, though we had suspected that he was because he came from a Christian home. He had denied Christ for six months. But he heard me speaking with the colonel. Then he came to me later that evening and confessed, and we prayed together.

"The others who were there were almost ready to revolt because they considered I had not been dealt with fairly, but I persuaded them not to. This led to much conversation about faith and why it is important.

"Then a few days later we were back in our barracks and I had to report to administration that I was back from the military school. "Why didn't you make the grade?" asked the administrator. "Because I didn't pass the political exam," I replied as he looked through my papers. "Give me your documents," he said, "you are promoted." I looked at him. "Yes, you're promoted." he said. He was of a much lower rank than the colonel, but God had used this little fellow. God stood with me and promoted me!

Daniel shot me a look of comic astonishment—eyebrows high, forehead furrowed, a quirky smile working his mouth—he had been deliberately reprieved. God's acts in our lives often leave us astonished.

"Before the army I went through a crisis,—Daniel continued—*I didn't know if my faith was real or just like a play in a theatre. Then when I went to the army I had prayed that God would give me such situations so that I would know if it was for real. He answered those prayers. There were several difficult times when I said that I believed and it was hard for me, but God always brought good out of it for me.*

"Every time I was sent to another posting I had to confess Christ. In fact I had to confess him every day. It was not enough to do so only once. I know that it can be difficult, but I also know that it is never impossible to speak or work for God. He is always in and above our situation to give us wisdom and help.

"In those difficult times it was not usually possible to travel abroad or to arrange larger Christian camps for young people, but we constantly held smaller ones in summer houses, at a mill or in boats on a lake. There were always opportunities to meet, to share testimonies and to inspire one another.

"Another difficulty was that there was only one Protestant Faculty of Theology in Prague with only 30 students allowed, just a very few from each denomination. Our Church could only send one student each year. Then an illegal course started up—Bible Education by Extension. We gathered ten to twelve students, though no diplomas were ever awarded.

"Today we have freedom. The church can do as she pleases—but does she do more than she used to? It seems to me that she does almost the same as she always did! It depends on the individuals, on people who want to work for the Lord, not on the system, communist or any other. Those who used to say they could do nothing because of the communists still do nothing!

"After grammar school I studied for two years at a medical opticians college in Brno. I am an optometrist. What gives me much joy is that a person has vision, and, though God does not always

give everything we might hope for, he is faithful and he does not forget our little faithfulnesses.

"After training as an optometrist I was invited to pastor the congregation in Veselí while working in my profession. I worked in Veselí for seven years, and there was much hard physical work at the church because it needed rebuilding, but only one person was converted, and then he returned to the world because of his girlfriend. Although we had many testimonies and we renovated the church building no-one came to Christ.

"Then we thought we should make a move, and came here to Tábor. We prayed that we should serve Christ, but if it continued as in Veselí we thought maybe something was not right in our lives, and that we were being a brake on God's work. And God replied by giving us a little revival in our church! Outsiders came in. We didn't do it, we helped, but God did it. God worked in their lives as they were ready for change. Now about half of our congregation are new people, some young and some older. The first seven years we were faithful in the work. God saw it and blessed us in these last eight years, so we see that it is the work of God's Holy Spirit, and not man's work. We are just like little players in his great plan.

"Revival came at the time of political change. God had given us the idea of holding Christian musical evenings. We invited different music groups from November to March. The second Saturday in each month we had a concert. We invited our friends, did all the preparations, and then the group would come. We had our first concert the week before the Velvet Revolution—on December 17, 1989. It had already been organised, and we could suddenly invite everyone through the press and put up notices, which would not have been allowed before. Many people came and heard testimonies. The preparations had been going on for almost a year.

"Our speaker was Jiří Grygar. He's a famous Czech astronomer. His theme was 'The Big Bang and The Bible'. One month after the Revolution he was with us and we couldn't get all the people in to hear about the Bible being the word of God. His testimony was so powerful. Because he is so very erudite, well-known, and often on TV, people thought highly of him and were moved to come to church.

"Then Josef Potoček, the mayor of Hradec Králové and a member

of our church, gave a lecture on 'Evolution and the Bible' which people found very interesting. By this time people had learnt to come into the church, so we could organise other events for them and they would come to 'musical services'. If we had only thought of this after the Revolution it would have been too late, but we had it all prepared in time—for God's right time! These evenings lasted for five years before we realised that we should close them down. Now people weren't coming to hear the gospel, but just for a free concert. We thought it dangerous for the church to continue as a custom or tradition what God had blessed in the past. We knew we needed to find a new way to reach people.

"Now in these new times, not just after the Revolution, we need a new way to come close to our people, and we are searching for this new way. Work for the Lord is always fresh and challenging like this. Our church services continue, and we are still engaged in training students through the Bible Education by Extension programme, but the musical mission work took a lot of time and money. Since the Revolution people have become very materialistic, and we need to reach out to them. We do still have the occasional concert, and we are planning a music club to be led by two boys who have been converted and who were playing heavy metal."

Marta Holeková of Prague told me about the difficulties she experienced as a Christian in communist times in Czechoslovakia:

"Even in Secondary School I invited some of my class mates who had become good friends to our church youth group. I didn't do it publicly, but I invited individual girls when I felt it was safe. We would never talk openly about what we were doing, because it was dangerous to pass on such information. Even before I became a new-born Christian I always tried to draw people closer to the influence of the Lord.

"I became a Christian in 1969, in the spring when I was in England. When the Russians came into Prague in 1968 I was not there, I was working at a Christian Bible school in England. I saw many differences. The faith was the same, but being there enriched my spiritual life.

"Later, in the 70's, when I was back in Czechoslovakia, during the summers we would arrange youth camps. We went to a cottage in the country, and we had Bible teaching. But it all had to be done secretly—it couldn't be done officially, but only at someone's home or country cottage. Although we had wonderful and encouraging experiences we could never talk about any of them when strangers were present.

"During those difficult years people in the West discovered that we would be willing to accept Christian literature. We often had a lot arrive, and had to distribute it. We gave parcels to different Christians, or they would come and take it—many Bibles, concordances, Bible dictionaries and children's Bibles. Many came from Holland where I had also worked later in 1969. The people who brought them I consider to be very, very courageous. It was so dangerous for them to cross the border into Czechoslovakia. We met many such people, but we did not learn their names because we met them only at night. The Lord gave us great confidence for this work, and it never happened that we were betrayed.

"We really did not have enough Bibles. I well remember when I got my first Bible. It was from my grandfather, who was a pastor. That Bible was very old, and damaged from bombing in the war. We couldn't go and buy a Bible. There were only available what people already had. Later in the 70's they did publish some Bibles and theological books, one or two, but it was not nearly enough.

"After I had received that old Bible I was so glad to have it. Then later some friends of my father had a Bible which they left for me. I gave the old Bible to one of my friends, and she was so glad. She was not a Christian, but I'm sure she was reading it.

"When I was in Holland I was once in a meeting with Corrie ten Boom. She asked me to come to the front, and she prayed for me and for my ministry in front of the whole meeting. That was a very powerful experience for me. She prayed for me and for my ministry and for the Lord's presence in my life. I felt the presence of the Lord, and I believe it really had a strong influence in my life."

With great difficulty Igor André, then a medical student and now a consultant cardiologist, travelled to Mittersill from Bratislava, the capital of Slovakia the eastern part of Czechoslovakia, in the summer of 1975. I met him in May, 1997, in Vavrišovo, a village in the foothills of the Slovak Tatra Mountains. The years rolled back as he told me how much his visit to Mittersill had meant to him 22 years earlier.

"It was a wonder to get to Mittersill because at that time we needed permission from what seemed like about sixteen different authorities! They were in three categories. First you had to receive an allocation of foreign currency from the bank, and there was no guarantee of money being available. When we received it, it seemed to us like a huge sum of money. Secondly you needed permission from your school or work place, including from the Socialist Union of Youth in the University, and third from the police before you could get your passport. It took over six months to arrange all of this.

"If we wanted to go the very first thing we needed was an invitation from friends in Austria. I didn't have any friends there, but Alex fixed it up for me. It was somewhat anonymous, as we never did visit those friends who invited us!

"To begin with I was just very excited, as it was the very first time in my life that I could travel to any western country. I was aged 20 and a student of medicine. I went with Josef Bán, and we travelled by train to Zell-am-See from where we were collected, and taken to Mittersill—to share a room with a group of six American boys.

"Secondly, I remember so very well first experiencing that Christianity is international. We met people from so many countries in that camp. At that time occasionally one person would come to Slovakia to visit us—but we'd never met black Christian people at all. Some were from South Africa, others from Germany, from France and so on. There was that amazing feeling that we were brothers and sisters together. We from Slovakia had never known anything like it before. People in authority here told us that we were a small minority with no hope and that Christianity was dying out. Then in Mittersill we found a new perspective, we experienced a huge Christian family and found that so very encouraging.

"Thirdly, I remember being impressed by the healthy spirit in the camp. It was based on biblical education, conversations, hymns

and songs and free time with sports and games. It struck us as being all very well organised. We came with no experiences of any larger camps, because we couldn't even have Christian camps for Slovaks at home. We felt thrilled to be part of this large camp. We had thought we'd stay for just a week, and then go to visit friends of my family in Switzerland. But after a couple of days we decided to stay to the end of the camp in Mittersill. Our friends called us from Switzerland and couldn't understand why we had put off travelling on to them.

"Now, in 1997, it is the second year that I'm organising a Christian camp for young people here in Vavrišovo. Mittersill was a pattern for me. The language is different, but my aim is the same. People ask me how I learnt to organise such a camp! After breakfast we have a quiet time just as we did in Mittersill, when I remember reading the first letter of Peter for half an hour alone with the Lord. That was so good. We might invite a group to come to sing to us—as I recall how well those Americans sang in their group and that was so encouraging with Marilyn Knapp leading the singing. I also invite outside preachers to visit us for a couple of days. The Holy Spirit has enabled me to change the orientation of young people.

"The camp in Mittersill was only for two weeks, and it was only for Christians, but I rank it as being one of the ten most important events in my life—it changed the whole motivation for my future Christian life. And not for mine only—I know of many people who are still active for Christ all over the world because of Mittersill!

"Perhaps the most important aspect of Mittersill for us was the excellent biblical teaching we received. At that time we had almost no biblical literature available in Slovak—it was forbidden or illegal. In Mittersill, Walter and Ingrid Trobisch gave us excellent biblical teaching on marriage and relationships. It was superb preparation for life.

"Then there was teaching about mission for students and young people—how we could witness to our fellow students and serve them. We had good materials provided and good small groups in which to discuss the topics. It was wonderful that we ourselves could speak about evangelism, and that made the discussion so real.

"The day before we left we had the Lord's supper, and that

brought many of us into a new experience with our Lord. We knew that he is still living, that he is great, and that he could fill us and use our lives in the future.

"Now I am a cardiologist. I work in the coronary care unit in the University Hospital in Bratislava. I am married, with two sons, and I also lead a charitable work through a church mission called Bethany which has five social work projects in Slovakia. We work among old people, and have 15 old folk in our care home. We also care for old people in their own homes. Then we have a sheltered home for 20 mentally handicapped adults at Senec near Bratislava. We also have, under reconstruction, a nursing home for 20 to 30 people including drug addicts at Kalinovo, beyond Zvolen, and finally we have our Bethany Centre in Bratislava. Here we keep in contact with other charities, we organise seminars giving teaching on developments in Christian social work to members of the different Churches. Bethany is a charity of the Brethren Church, but we have contacts in Germany, in Switzerland and in the United Kingdom. We set it up in 1991, and now have 35 employees, mostly Christians. None of this was possible under communism.

"I also work with teenagers, as my boys are in their teens. We meet every Sunday, and have summer camps for 40 to 50 of them here in Vavrišovo. It is like a little Mittersill, because the studying years are crucial for them—they set the direction for the whole of their lives.

"When I returned from Mittersill in 1975 I had been given material, papers and so on from the course. I was so afraid that the customs would find them and make trouble for me at my university that I finally threw them out of the train window. Later, two or three days after John Stott visited us, the secret police, the Š.T.B., called a student friend of mine in to their office. They asked him a few stupid questions about his contacts in England. They wanted to make trouble for him at his technical university. Now we can laugh, but at the time it was really frightening. Even Catholic students could find they were dismissed from the university because of their Christian activities."

Student visits often took a good deal of arranging from the

Austrian end. Anikó and I spent a whole November one year, early on in our ministry, touring Austria to ensure that each East European student who had been invited had a reliable family to visit. We looked for a family with children, pets, a grandmother and a garden to talk about back home to the chaps at security! But then what joy and sense of almost triumph over the 'system' when they arrived in Mittersill for a couple of weeks! There they would learn more about the Bible and how the Gospel is relevant to students today. They would think through different methods of personal and group evangelism, often based on evangelistic Bible studies. Most importantly they would discover that their little corner was not alone in being difficult, but that God had people in many little corners of his world and was also at work in other, perhaps much harder places.

We never knew how long we would have to do this work. Many feared a return to a harsher stalinistic regime but in fact the authorities gradually allowed slightly more freedom.

Niusia Alphonsus from Wrocław, Poland, writes about a wonderful opening of her eyes which happened shortly before the stringent clampdown under martial law declared in Poland on 13th December 1981:

"In 1981 I was given the opportunity to be part of a students' camp in Mittersill. The fellowship with Christians of many different backgrounds and cultures, and the lectures on the Book of Amos which portrays God as the sovereign God of history, helped me to become aware of the fact that God's children are all over the world. It also helped me to discern what was biblical and what was cultural in my own life."

Our work in the countries of Eastern Europe with their long established if somewhat nominal churches was easy in comparison with the much less fertile soil of North Africa, for example, where the Church hardly has a foothold. Sometimes we were able to get students from different local churches in the same country or even the same town to meet in Mittersill and that was when things really started to happen. A small group can be so much more effective than the sum of its individual members. We trained them, taught them, befriended and inspired them, and great things would happen when they returned home. God had joined them into closely knit teams. We were alongside them, we knew their families and friends, their pastors and churches.

It was at Mittersill that the vision was shared for a house where students could safely have their camps in Poland and another in the Czech Republic (at the time Czechoslovakia). It was while at Mittersill that the Hungarian students decided they wanted to work together and publish evangelistic literature to help their friends. It was at Mittersill where Croats would meet Serbs and Macedonians and where the seed was sown for a united Yugoslav theological training school, before the war came in 1990 and destroyed the buildings if not the vision!

I find it so humbling and yet so encouraging to look back now another ten years after the ending of the communist system in Europe to realise how faithful God has been. All over Eastern, (now Central) Europe, the students we found were, by and large, fresh converts, or even just interested in becoming Christians. Today many of them are leaders in different churches or counting for God in university or public life. How much training could we give them? By human standards, very little indeed. They became the 'Bare Foot Doctors', trained largely by another one who was himself no more trained in any formal sense and they in turn gathered their friends and shared the treasures of the Good News about Jesus their Lord and Saviour at a time and in an environment where it was virtually seditious to set up any meeting not approved by the state. Encouragement in the faith and friendship was what was on offer.

May I quote Niusia from Poland again:

"When I look back, I am grateful to the Lord that in spite of our numerous mistakes, immaturity and childish attitude to life the Lord used us as his weak vessels. Once, at school, I was talking to one of my classmates about the Gospel. At that time she seemed to show little enthusiasm or interest in the things of God. So how surprised I was when, a few days later, she herself expressed a desire to take

part in our Christian camp at Bielice. Such a decision stirred up not only the curiosity but also the opposition of our predominantly Catholic classmates. A few weeks later the Lord gave me the greatest joy in my life—seeing people's lives being transformed by the power of God's grace. Over the next few months, God touched the hearts of three more girls in our class. Such a sudden flow of conversions naturally made not only the parents but also the teachers worry about these 'poisonous trends'. In spite of all the difficulties we decided to meet for prayer before classes. This time of fellowship with the Lord and with each other proved to be an immense encouragement for our future walk with God.

"Later the Lord gave us opportunities to witness to our teachers. One of them, who also happened to be the headmaster of the school and a real communist (there were never very many of them in Poland) engaged us in long debates about Christianity. He and his family even came to one of our camps in the mountains, and though he did not confess Christ at that time, I believe the seed of God's word was sown in his heart and that one day he will be called into God's kingdom.

"Where do we stand now, ten years after our conversions? Marzenka, the first to be found by the Lord, is a translator at the Bible Seminary in Wrocław, Poland, while during the vacations she and her husband are active spreading the Gospel in Siberia. Viola married, moved to the north of Poland and is a member of the church in Gdańsk. Agnieszka works in a bank and also has a counselling ministry. Sadly, one married a non-believer and slid back. And me? I married a Tamil and live in Mannar, in north west Sri Lanka where I teach English and through this try to witness to the community."

Students who came to Austria quickly realised they could arrange evangelistic or Bible teaching camps in their own countries and thus reach far more student friends with far less language barrier problems than are posed by an international conference.

As IFES staff we had our regular reporting and discussion sessions with Stacey, both at Mittersill and in Lausanne. Stacey had a priceless gift in that he spent enormous time and effort ensuring that he elicited the best contribution from all his staff. Few probably knew his denominational affiliation. He did not know every country and situation in great detail, but because of his wide experience in North America and from his visits around the world, God enabled him to home in on our difficulties and joys with immense insight. We in turn were inspired to do the same with all those in our care.

The summer conferences at Mittersill provided us all with first-rate teaching, Bible exposition and formal training in evangelism, but more than that it gave us as staff time to sit down or walk out on a free day and discuss with each of our people the areas where they felt they were doing particularly well and developing their gifts, and other areas where they felt the need for help or room for improvement. No records were ever kept of these discussions, but they were most valuable in helping students to reflect on their situations. Almost every year there were one or two who felt that a full time course at a Bible college would really help them in their service for the Lord. Then I would try to facilitate whatever the students requested to develop them as people fit to serve their Lord. We found that students were capable of great responsibilities if given the encouragement and opportunity.

We even managed to invite non-Christians to Mittersill—though that was not our primary intention—but God was wonderfully at work. Mihael Jonke came as a student from Zagreb in Yugoslavia. He writes:

"Mittersill, Mittersill! It seems so long ago, but I can say with all my heart before the Lord, that for me personally, many foundational things actually started there. Probably you even didn't know that I received assurance of my salvation there, something that was tormenting me for years. I simply couldn't believe that it is all free and that I could really be a child of God. It was there sitting on that well in the middle of that courtyard, where I spoke with one of the leaders about my fears and doubts about my salvation. Suddenly the Lord gave me a vision. I saw myself as though from behind just smoothly entering through big heavy iron gates that had been opened long before— and I was in! This picture that the Lord

gave me there and then was total release from the bondage of not knowing for sure that I belonged to God and his Kingdom of Grace.

"Apart from that I can list at least ten leaders that are in full-time Christian ministry now who went with me, year after year, three times in all, to Mittersill summer conferences and received a solid foundation for their personal faith and ministry.

"I want to say a big "Thank you in Jesus' name!" to IFES and all who have been involved in many ways in the ministry to many groups of Christians from the former Yugoslavia, and from Croatia where we now live and continue to work for the Lord."

Mihael Jonke came from a Protestant family in strongly Catholic Croatia. Poland, likewise is strongly Catholic. Typically in Polish Roman Catholicism the Blessed Virgin Mary is very important, and appears with the infant Jesus on her knee. Prayers are generally offered to Mary, the Mother of God. Jesus is either a helpless babe in arms, or a dead corpse hanging limply from a cross. The resurrection is almost conspicuous by its absence. Polish Catholics could be said to have largely got stuck on Good Friday, instead of moving on to the triumph of Easter Sunday.

Some Polish Roman Catholics are truly afraid of reading the Bible for themselves. The priest may well tell them that they might come to the wrong conclusions, and an error in interpretation is a serious sin in Catholic teaching. So it is a common notion that it is better not to read the Bible yourself, but just trust in the priest's interpretation. This is particularly true in the country and in small towns in Poland, despite several millions of Catholic Bibles having been printed and distributed and despite biblical revival movements, notably Oasis, having been at work particularly since the 1970s amongst many hundreds of thousands of Catholic young people.

So what is happening in the Catholic Church in Poland today? Perhaps the greatest changes have been the change from the use of Latin to the local language in their services, but also very importantly there has been the translation of the Bible into modern Polish. This was published in 1966. To many Catholics the Bible is still just revered as a holy object, but to increasing numbers it is again open to be read and presents a challenge to them to live according to its teaching.

There have been various renewal movements in the Roman Catholic Church in recent years, one of the most noteworthy being, perhaps, Oasis, also known as 'Light and Life'. This arose as a result of the influence of a Catholic priest, Franciszek Blachnicki and was based at Krościenko, an idyllic spot in the hills south of Cracow close to the Polish border with Slovakia. It was under the protection of Karol Wojtyła (then cardinal in Cracow before he was elected as Pope) in the 1960's, grew remarkably in the 1970's, and sought to bring the Bible into the daily life of the laity. Many hundreds of thousands of young Poles have been touched by Oasis through camps and home Bible study groups. They still have processions to honour Mary. "Polish Catholicism' s proverbial devotion to the Virgin Mary has been retained and cultivated within the movement. This strong Marian overtone," writes Grażyna Sikorska ("Light and Life" page 69), "was of course indigestible to the Polish Protestants." However, despite their huge loyalty to Mary, Bible reading Catholic charismatics are increasingly becoming a force within the Roman Church.

"After 1976, writes Grażyna Sikorska, the centrality of evangelism in the Oasis programme led Father Blachnicki to establish contacts with Protestant evangelistic groups including "Campus Crusade for Christ"—an American-based interdenominational movement known also as "Agape"... Agape concentrates on preaching the basic Christian truths common to all denominations and aims at helping individuals to establish a personal relationship with Jesus, accepting him as the Saviour and Lord. Those who become believers are then encouraged to join a local church of their choice in order to continue their spiritual growth through further instruction within the local Christian community. Agape's aims fitted in perfectly with Father Franciszek's ideas of the best way to introduce young people to the movement (Oasis) and its secondary training programme...He was also very impressed with (Agape's) readiness to adapt their programmes to suit denominational and local religious tradition.

"In 1975 he decided on an unprecedentedly close form of cooperation with Campus Crusade for Christ in his programme for the evangelization of Poland. In the summer of 1976 representatives of the Agape movement arrived in Poland at the invitation of Father Blachnicki, to lead special evangelisation sessions at several of the Oasis retreats. Since 1977 Agape members have been participating in the New Life Oasis—run according to a new evangelistic programme." "Youth with a Mission" also became involved, "mainly by preparing group leaders."

"Father Franciszek's down-to-earth cooperation with non-Catholic movements as well as his enthusiasm for such cooperation alarmed the more conservative sections of the Catholic clergy and the Episcopate. Father Franciszek was accused of trying to protestantise the movement... A special Church commission was set up to investigate the accusations. Among its appointed members were Bishop Władysław Miziołek (Chairman of the Commission for Ecumenism) and Cardinal Karol Wojtyła of Cracow. Father Blachnicki defended himself, and all charges were dropped, but soon after his death in February, 1987, and with Karol Wojtyła away as pontiff in Rome it was not long before those conservative sections of the Catholic clergy quietly divided Oasis by having it administered locally in each diocese, and ruled so as to attempt to close it down. Yet survive it does. Only time will show what God will do with it."[16]

In the communist era the Roman Catholic Church represented the only permitted opposition to the government, and ideologists of the Communist Party sought to discredit Blachnicki and smash the "Light-Life" movement. The communist authorities had good reason to fear "Light-Life", not only because as many as half the young priests in Poland had come from within its ranks, and half a million Poles participated in its summer "Oasis" camps but particularly because of the uncompromising and dynamic Christianity displayed by the movements members. As such it seemed to be astonishingly strong, and its political strength grew with the election of Karol Wojtyła to the papacy on 16th October, 1978. Today there has been a shake-out of those who were in the Church for the wrong, i.e. political reasons, but the Church is still a force to be reckoned with. Only now are younger priests from the charismatic movement beginning to rise in the hierarchy. Could we see a new Biblical reformation sweep the Catholic Church in Poland over the next 50 to 100 years? My prayer is that, given time, it will.

Jesus said: "The kingdom of heaven is like a mustard seed, which a man took and planted in his field. Though it is the smallest of all your seeds, yet when it grows, it is the largest of garden plants and becomes a tree, so that the birds of the air come and perch in its branches." Matt 13,31-32.

Witold Chrapek came to Mittersill as a student from Poland. He was born into a typical Roman Catholic family. They adhered to the Roman Catholic Church and its traditions. His parents never taught him and his brother about God or the Lord Jesus, and they never read the Bible—in fact there was no Bible in the home. Witold recalls:

"In my student years I stopped going to church, but towards the end of my studies in Cracow I met Alex Williams, an Englishman who was studying at the same technical university and who was a Christian. Alex invited me to a local Baptist church once or twice, and though I liked it there I decided that was not for me. Life with all its sinful pleasures seemed to be so attractive!

"After graduating in 1968 I commenced working in my profession as an electrical engineer. About the same time I began to learn English as I had long wanted to travel abroad, and I knew I had to master the language first. Some two years later I wrote to Alex Williams, as he was the only person living in the West I knew at that time, and asked him about the possibility of visiting England for a month or so to practise my English. I wanted to go in the summer of 1971. In his reply Alex said he wouldn't be at home that summer. He proposed that I should join him at a youth camp in Austria as that would give an excellent opportunity to practise my English. Everyone there would speak English.

"I was excited with this possibility as I had never been to the West before. Alex sent me an official invitation and a ticket. I needed these to get both my Polish passport and the Austrian visa.

At that time, being single and educated, I had every chance of being refused a passport, as there was the risk that young people like me, when they found themselves in the West, might choose to stay there. But I got both, and that summer I found myself at a youth camp in Schloß Mittersill, Austria.

"As Alex had told me, there were many young people from all over the world, and they all spoke English. It was a Christian Bible camp, so I had to attend morning and afternoon Bible studies, lectures etc. It was the first time I had been exposed to the Word of God to such an extent, and in the mirror of it I saw my life as dirty and lacking. God's Spirit convicted me of my sin and I wanted to change my life. Not being fully instructed in how to go about it I tried to change my life by my own efforts in the months that followed. Of course I failed, until I realised that I had to submit my whole life to the Lord Jesus to have victory over sin and temptation.

"I had the privilege to be in Schloß Mittersill again in the summer of 1972, and by that time I was already a different person. It was then that I met Mr Ernst F Bolten with his family and we became friends. It was Ernst's uncle John Bolten who, in 1967, had been instrumental in helping purchase the castle to be a Christian training centre. Through Ernst's help and sponsorship and by God's grace I was able to travel to the States in the summer of 1973. I sold my car to pay for the fare, but my long-desired dream came true.

"A month or two after my arrival in the USA a Pittsburgh based engineering and construction company signed a multi-million dollar contract with the Polish Government to design and build an iron foundry in central Poland. As they were looking for bilingual engineers to work on the project I could only marvel at and thank God for his providence that I was there at that time. For the next three years I worked for that company and they were the best years of my professional life.

"While in Pittsburgh I had warm and happy Christian fellowship at a Christian and Missionary Alliance Church where I was also baptized. After I returned to Poland in 1976 I joined a small denomination which today is called the Church of Free Christians,

a Polish version of the English Open Brethren. My knowledge of English now helps me to serve as an interpreter to English speaking preachers and teachers who visit our assemblies. I am currently secretary of our local assembly in Bielsko-Biała and also a deputy chairman of our Church Council."

So much for a non-Christian's visit to Mittersill! It was an enormous privilege for us staff workers, all of us foreigners, to be taken into the hearts of those we sought to encourage in the Lord. We were accepted by them. Despite all our shortcomings we were used by God and we could see his fruit growing in their lives. What more could anyone ask?

IFES always had the somewhat strange notion of supporting the students in the work that *they* felt God was calling *them* to do rather than using them to implement some grand plan conceived by some mission board or committee in a foreign land. Of course we might have introduced ideas or they might have picked up ideas which worked well in other countries (we hoped they would), but we were very conscious that they were the ones who would have to answer to the authorities and take the responsibility for their actions. Not surprisingly the pay-off in terms of involvement and commitment was immense at the time, while many are still in full-time or part-time Christian service now, many years later!

Milenko Andjelić, from Belgrade, Serbia, came to England after a course at Mittersill. When we took him to All Nations Christian College the staff asked if Anikó was his wife! He was only 18 and not married at that time. Since then he has been blessed with a wonderful wife, Snežana, and two fine sons. After a Law degree in Belgrade, and a master's degree in Mission at Wheaton, Milenko worked for his doctorate in Theology at Münster, Germany. He had hoped to teach at a united Yugoslav evangelical seminary, before the war shattered that dream in 1992. He worked on the legal side of obtaining the many permissions needed for their Pentecostal Church in Belgrade to be rebuilt. It is now called, significantly, Belgrade Evangelical Church. Milenko writes:

"When Alex and Anikó first visited our family in Belgrade in

1970 they were newly-married and I attended high school. I admired their friendliness which eventually led to a stay in their home in England, and following that Inter-Schools Christian Fellowship camps, Mittersill with the IFES and All Nations Christian College in later years. The value of this experience was in my growing sense of Christian unity around the Lordship of Jesus Christ. I was from a godly but relatively closed Christian group in Belgrade, but have learned to benefit from and enjoy fellowship with Christians of other traditions."

CHASING CHRISTIANS, CHASING BIRDS

I do not ever recall having difficulties with any fellow members of the IFES staff, but working with people does entail the risk of trouble, and perhaps especially so in Christian work. After all, we are in the business of asking people to change, to allow Jesus Christ to mend their broken lives, to put the pieces back together, to grow more Christlike. Some people may have a different idea of what real change is. If we never had trouble with people there would be something quite wrong—we would all be in a bad rut together, none of us ever changing for the better! Handling change, or handling trouble with people, is part of the challenge of Christian work.

As visitors to Eastern Europe my wife and I often felt that we had an advantage. We could not be on one side or the other of any local squabbles or differences of opinion—denominational or personal. How fortunate to be able to claim just to be Christians, (or 'English Anglicans' if the need arose!) This became particularly helpful when the charismatic movement arrived on the scene in Eastern Europe. We even knew what to expect, because we had had to work through the issues a few years earlier in England. We had seen our own churches taking sides, denominations dividing and congregations splitting over what was, especially at the beginning, quite a divisive issue.

In Hungary, and in Poland in particular, we were the peacemakers, if at all possible, or at least the go-betweens among different groups of students in different churches who had worked together so enthusiastically before but were now seemingly at loggerheads. Surely, we thought, it was really the work of the devil himself to divide the small groups of Christians and get them to fight one another. Otherwise they would have been able to see that, even if they did differ over a few matters, it was far better to fight together for Christ and against the powers of darkness in the lives of complete non-believers.

The divisions were gradually becoming less troublesome by the end of the 1970s. Billy Graham's crusades in several East European countries around this time also greatly helped by giving a good focus to co-operative evangelism. Many students, especially those who had not been Christians themselves for long, took the lead in reconciling Lutherans and Pentecostals, Methodists and Baptists.

The summer conferences in Mittersill were also our main staff meetings. Those were the days when the staff concerned with Eastern Europe were relatively few in number. Although by 1976 Christine Davies had joined me from the staff of the British student work linked to IFES called UCCF (Universities and Colleges Christian Fellowship) where she had been working in the struggling colleges' Christian Unions in England, we were not, in fact, a particularly Anglo-centric bunch. A very dear Danish couple, Arne and Ingeborg Kappelgaard, studied at a seminary in Bucharest and took charge in Romania. Later, a very talented Dutch colleague, Anne-Marie Kool, began to work in Hungary and to this day continues to teach mission and bring a remarkably good influence to bear on the student work in Hungary.

When we met at Mittersill it was not to congratulate each other on the fine job we were doing, but to help one another in the thick of the battle! Looking back I think we would have been wise to have given ourselves more time to 'active dreaming'. We could have dreamt of the future, prayerfully devising our strategies. But we were busy nurturing seed corn among the future student leaders; they would bear a rich future harvest. We were aiming for effective collaboration to utilise IFES's strengths and resources to best effect. Chris Davies and I certainly created an axis of co-ordinated effort, and involved other staff and expertise in Eastern Europe wherever we could on the widest basis, from Austria to Spain, from the U.K. to Scandinavia.

The development of even limited strategic aims gave us a shared view of what we were aiming for under God and drew us together tremendously as a team. Eastern Europe was gradually changing and we were neither afraid to change nor to make change happen! The real challenge is to keep things changing and devise new and better ways of doing things when everything is going well and the situation is stable.

The choice of speakers for Mittersill was crucially important. Exposure there to our selected student leaders meant that, if they were favourably impressed, they could be invited to extend their ministries into Poland, Hungary or Yugoslavia. Several times this strategy worked wonderfully well, with considerable blessing to far more students than we could ever have gathered in Austria.

Some of those speakers were also helpful Christian writers. As they shared their books the idea grew for not only spreading good existing Christian literature in translation in Eastern Europe, but also for encouraging local authors, students and pastors to translate and to write. Publishing inside Eastern Europe was difficult if not impossible at this time, but the seeds were being sown.

At city student meetings, evangelistic conferences, country camps and theological colleges, the church leaders of tomorrow were addressed by some of Europe's brightest Bible expositors. Julian Charley travelled from Liverpool to Debrecen in eastern Hungary, a centre of Reformed scholarship to help theological students, some of whom today are members of the Fellowship of Evangelical European Theologians. Julian also took the gospel to Croatia and inspired them to share the good news with their fellow students. The two students who organised this holiday camp are both now pastors of churches in Zagreb.

John Stott, with his leadership and vision was a great contributor to building up the work. Though not on IFES staff he often acted as an honorary senior staff member. John was enormously encouraging, great fun to be with and amazingly well informed and erudite on a huge range of subjects. He toured Eastern Europe more than once, visiting at different times Romania, Hungary, Poland, Czechoslovakia[17] and Yugoslavia. Everyone appreciated his quick wit, deep learning and also his love of the richly varied bird life in the different countries. Each bird species makes its own wildlife habitat—much like the varied human cultures. Poland is strongly Roman Catholic but with an enthusiastic Protestant minority; Czechoslovakia was mainly Catholic but influenced by the Hussite and later reformations; and Hungary is two thirds Catholic and one third Protestant. Romania is largely Orthodox but with significant Protestant minorities, while Yugoslavia was strongly Orthodox (Serbia) or strongly Catholic (Croatia and Slovenia) or Muslim (Macedonia and Bosnia Hercegovina) with no more than a sprinkling of any Protestants anywhere.

It amused John Stott that there were so many languages in Yugoslavia. At that time you could attend primary school in any one of 12 languages, depending on which part of the country you lived in. You could then proceed to secondary school in one of seven languages and after that you could go on to study at university in one of four languages. Secondary education could be in Slovene or Croatian, Serbian, Hungarian, Romanian, Macedonian or Albanian! Arguments were probable between such unlikely bedfellows. As we know, they eventually went to war with one another.

My first contact with John Stott had been through a tape-recorded message, played to #100 or so members of the Leeds University Christian Union. This was in November 1965, at a preparatory meeting in the church hall of St Augustine's, Wrangthorn, for what turned out to be quite a fruitful mission to Leeds University which John was shortly to lead. He arrived in February 1966 for the mission and my task was to carry his wellington boots. At that time Leeds was famous for its sticky mud as well as its green pea-soup fogs, or 'smogs' when smoke was mixed with fog and when, if you stretched your arm out in front of you, you could barely see your hand. It was a good introduction and my perk for carrying the boots was to have him speak at a meeting in my room in my residence, Boddington Hall, to my overseas student friends.

I had been having weekly Bible studies with another Englishman, a Gibraltarian who was nominal Roman Catholic, and an Icelander, Magnús Kristinsson, who lodged right above me, a nominal Lutheran. To my great joy Magnús, along with quite a number of other students, was wonderfully converted in the mission John Stott led. Magnús first taught English and German at a school in Akureyri on Iceland's north coast, but has spent time recently studying the teaching of German as a foreign language in Stuttgart.

From Leeds I moved on to my post-graduate apprenticeship in Refractories at the Academy of Mining and Metallurgy in Cracow, which was good preparation for my next assignment, on IFES staff in Eastern Europe. There I was to meet John Stott much more often and in a great variety of situations. These included international student Bible courses organised by IFES at Oak Hill College in London in 1977, as well as at Mittersill in Austria. With a twinkle in his eye, and allowing me now to call him 'Uncle John', he carefully prepared me for the trips we were to make together to the different East European countries, advising on the purchase of a pair of binoculars and a copy of 'H, F&P' Heinzel, Fitter and Parslow's 'Birds of Britain and Europe'. Bird-watching became great fun, and led to many amusing incidents even though it was only a bit of relaxation which never took precedence over our gospel work.

In 1980 I wrote some notes into my copy of H,F&P: 'Collared Dove—Streptopelia decaocto, Donji Miholjac, Yugoslavia 11.4.1980'. I had set off with my elder son, David, then eight, to Zagreb to visit Christian student friends—many of them now in full time Christian ministry—before taking the train to the tourist town of Bled. Ominously our train crossed Tito's funeral train on its way to Belgrade. Bled is an idyllic spot. A small island on which a castle is built is set in a deep blue lake surrounded by steep mountains. The spring air was warm and pale purple crocuses were emerging under the pine trees. After a day admiring this internationally famous beauty spot another train took us on to Graz in Austria, where David tended the sheep and partook of a kind Austrian friend's apple pie while improving his German! I returned to Zagreb and picked up a hire car just in time to meet Uncle John off his flight from London.

The idea was to travel by car to Novi Sad in Vojvodina, where there was a Baptist seminary and where an important meeting of evangelicals was to take place. John would speak and a Yugoslav Evangelical Alliance was to be inaugurated. Donji Miholjac was en route, a small almost insignificant, settlement on the banks of the river Drava, hard on the Hungarian border. Most people would not give the a place a second glance, but when you travel with John Stott be prepared to spend plenty of time patiently waiting in unusual places—under bushes, among reeds, but particularly in marshy places watching for, listening for, praying for a glimpse of what you and I might think is an ordinary pigeon, but what is in fact pointed out to you as a fine example of Streptopelia decaocto, the Collared Dove.

I must confess to being mildly amused, but also curiously fascinated by the huge variety and beauty of these feathered creatures. Donji Miholac is blessed with an overgrown sewage farm, or some such reedy boggy place down by the River Drava. We certainly heard Reed Warblers, though they are quite difficult to spot as they dart among the reeds. The meeting in Novi Sad had started by the time we arrived, but John seemed quite unperturbed, walked to the front and preached without batting an eye-lid.

It was worth going. The evangelicals in those parts, Croatia and Serbia now, were very few in number in a somewhat hostile environment and hence very suspicious of one another. Sometimes when visiting students or families in rural locations we would have to leave our car and walk. Many smaller roads were described as summer roads. Not made up, deeply rutted by horse drawn carts, marvellously muddy after rain, they could be impassable in a car at any time of year. We grew used to leaving the car and walking. Although Yugoslavia as we knew it then is no more, the churches have been working more together, and reaching out too in Bosnia Hercegovina in many towns where until the war there were no known evangelical Christians. Many of the Christian students I knew then are now in full-time service, pastoring churches, teaching theology, leading evangelism among Muslims and nominal Orthodox people. It was worth going to bring them together. Yugoslavs with their 12 languages were ethnically mixed and diverse. They would not have flocked to hear a Baptist or a Pentecostal speaker, but they flocked to hear an Anglican, a foreigner to all of them with no axe to grind, no enemies, only friends. We could all be brothers together because we are all one in Christ. They took John Stott to their hearts over that weekend and nicknamed him Tata Stotta—Father Stott!

After Yugoslavia we turned the car north toward Hungary. We crossed the Hungarian border near Szeged, and almost at once were both thrilled to see, resting on a low house roof, a Hoopoe (Upupa epops) with its long curved dark bill and prominent black-tipped crest, erected fan-wise. Plumage pinkish-cinnamon; tail and rounded wings strongly barred black and white so that in flight it looks like a huge round-winged black and white moth. Chief call a rapid far carrying clipped 'hoo-hoo-hoo'. We saw and heard and remember Upupa epops!

We drove past Szeged and settled down in another reed bed alongside the Fehér-tó (White Lake) where John was exuberantly pointing out to me my first sighting of an Avocet (Recurvirostra avosetta). I've seen plenty since, while cycling in Holland, but it is "unmistakable with its strikingly upcurved (recurved) bill, used with a side-to-side sweeping motion in feeding, and blue grey legs."(H,F&P) It stood there in the mud, hunting for its food, another of the wonders of God's good creation.

The Ornithological Society in Budapest was not very forthcoming, and neither was the British Consul on whom we paid a courtesy call. One afternoon however, we visited the Pasarét Reformed Church, where John spoke with their pastor, Cseri Kálmán, and to a group of theological students. We paid an evening visit to dr. Fabinyi Tibor a Lutheran lecturer in theology and a delightful pastor Széll Bulcsú, but our big break came through my wife's

Jóska bácsi, Uncle Jo, who lives in the small country town of Tamási, and who had connections.

In the communist world the right connections could get you groceries and meat from under the counter when none might be visibly available to common view. The right connections could get you a carpet, or bedding, or a slide projector or a holiday, almost anything in fact—and in this case the right introduction from Uncle Jo obtained for us the services of a young and enthusiastic local naturalist based in Kecskemét. He was superb, and guided us to the Ágasegyházai and Orgoványi salt lakes in the Orgovány Nature Reserve where we saw large numbers of geese. To me, as I suspect to most Hungarians, a goose is best when roast, but these were breeding colonies of the Greylag Goose, Anser anser, "One of the larger grey geese...orange bill and pink legs." H,F&P).

John Stott and I, however, feasted sumptuously on roast goose that evening in a tavern in Kecskemét with our naturalist friend. (I'm sure the menu just said goose, and we presumed we were eating domesticated goose, but it could have been a greylag for all I know!) It was well worth buying him that meal! The following day he had an idea. He remembered seeing where a large Black Woodpecker had been nesting the previous year. If, like Little Red Riding Hood on her way to visit grandmother, we were to creep through a wood and hide for a while in some bushes we might, just might... Of course, it was too exciting a prospect to be missed! We drove out the short distance to the wooded part of the Kiskunsági National Park near Bezsenyidűlő, passing several nesting pairs of White Storks, Ciconia ciconia, on lonely country house tops, some of them displaying their unusual courtship sign of "clattering mandibles together, at the same time as holding neck backwards in a U-bend."(H,F&P).

We parked the car and set off into the woods. We would have had very little chance without our guide, but after 10 or 15 minutes he motioned us to be silent, and to crouch down under some dead bracken or brambles behind a tree. The three of us were there for what seemed another quarter of an hour—in reality it was probably less—with our eyes fixed on a hole in a particular tree he had pointed out a few yards away. We were hoping to see the woodpecker emerge, but he suddenly arrived from one side, swooping in low up to his nest, displaying his typical very undulating flight. The Black Woodpecker, Dryocopus martius, is conspicuously large at18in/46cm and most distinctive, being the only large all-black land bird with his red crown and crest. He took one look at us with his strikingly bright yellow eye, let out a yelp and made off as fast as his wings could carry him!

Other memorable events of that trip to Hungary included seeing huge pink egrets wheeling above Velencei-tó (Lake Velencei). They were supposed to be Great White Egrets, Egretta alba, at 35 in (89 cm) much the largest of the white herons or egrets of the region but the setting sun gave them a gorgeous pink sheen. Earlier that day we had heard Serins, Serinus serinus, sweetly singing their jingling song like whispering Corn Buntings on the shore of Lake Balaton. Also, thanks to our naturalist friend, we managed to find a whole flock of Great Bustards, Otis tarda. "One of the largest (40in/102cm) land birds of the region, showing much white on black-tipped wings.. Male, substantially larger than female, has long moustachial bristles and rufous chestnut breast band."(H,F&P) I have read of other Englishmen going all the way to Hungary to shoot these famous Great Bustards, túzok in Hungarian—but that was before the Second World War when they were perhaps more plentiful, and certainly not, as now, rare and protected.

The following day we visited the town of Debrecen in Eastern Hungary. Debrecen is a centre of Reformed Church theological teaching and learning, but again I must confess that my memories are more to do with birds. We spent the night in an inn at Hortobágy out on the Puszta, the Great Hungarian Plain. I vividly recall a most embarrassing moment. I managed to lock the car with the keys inside it and John Stott looking on! Fortunately I was soon able to find a length of suitable wire and extricate both myself and the keys. We dined well on the famous Hungarian fish (goulash) soup and looked forward to visiting on the following day the Hortobágyi-halastó the fish lake from which the carp came to make the soup. We did not intend to search for fish, but to admire a special colony of nesting birds. In the morning I went off to the

Gents washroom for my shower, and was astonished to find, on my return, that John had also showered, though not in the Gents. But he wasn't the slightest bit embarrassed.

After breakfast, we departed for the fish lake. We needed to use a boat to reach the reedy island on which the colony of Spoonbills were nesting. The boat was kept by a warden. We found his house, but he was not at home. His young wife very touchingly brought out her telescope, set it up on its stand and searched the horizon—"Ah, yes! I see him coming!" she announced after a few moments. We could just discern a tiny speck slowly moving far out across the plain. We waited and waited, and the warden arrived and duly checked the permission we had been granted the previous day in Debrecen before unlocking his row boat. I rowed, and soon John was taking stunning photographs only a few yards from the nesting Spoonbills, Platalea leucorodia, large white heron-like birds with a long broad black bill, spoon shaped at the tip. The adults have a yellowish breast-band and in breeding season (which it very definitely was) a long golden yellow crest. I found them as amazing in reality as they subsequently appeared in John's photographs. (See "Birds our Teachers" by John Stott, Candle Books, U.K., 1999, page 73)

In 1984 I also travelled with John Stott to Romania. We left the hired car in Hungary, and crossed the border by train in order to save the usual horrendous car search the Romanian border guards regularly carried out. It was thrilling to witness the strength of the churches and hear of the bravery of the Christians. We arrived in Oradea, in Transylvania almost on the Hungarian border, and spring was bursting. But in the cold icy days of the winter, a couple of months previously, the pastor of the church, Paul Negruţ, a clinical psychologist and a hugely enthusiastic evangelist, pastor and leader, had found that someone had connected the high voltage cables, the feed for his power supply, to his drainpipe. He was supposed to clutch the drainpipe to steady himself on the ice, but mercifully he was not more than badly shaken by the electric shock as ice is not such a good conductor of electricity as is water. The authorities in Romania were still physically attacking the Church in such ways and also with staged road "accidents".

We were thrilled by the vision and fearless enthusiasm of a group of around 15 young leaders who met for several days' Bible teaching in a home. God was granting a measure of revival, and while the authorities refused permission for the churches to build, they could not stop people from coming to the services. Services were limited in number, but not in length, and the building was jam packed with hundreds of worshippers; loudspeakers carried the singing and preaching to those in the courtyard outside. The congregation totalled 2,500 in the morning and 3,000 in the evening—including the usual ten or so informers. Many young people were being swept by the Holy Spirit into the churches. John spoke at huge youth nurture groups, and one particular talk I vividly recall being an hour long overview of the whole Bible. They were as astounded as I was and lapped it all up.

But the birds were also calling—and astounding too when we caught sight of them! In the Danube Delta we were amazed by the White Pelicans, Pelecanus onocrotalus. My Birds of Britain and Europe describes them as "A very large heavy white bird, tinged pink and crested in breeding plumage; wing tips black, yellow patch on breast, bill bluish and pink, pouch pale pink or yellow, legs pink or orange... Flight majestic, with neck retracted; soars, glides and flies in formation." We saw them doing just that over the brackish coastal waters where they nest in the delta. Come to think of it, that could almost be the description of the Greater Crested Stott bird, fully regaled in brilliant white preaching robes over a black cassock with royal crest on flowing scarf; expounding the Bible with majestic flights of precisely chosen words, soaring, gliding over God's wonderful truths, flying in 'All Souls' formation along with vicars and curates and a fine accompanying multicoloured choir....

I also accompanied John Stott[18] to Poland in early 1987 for a well attended student conference over several days in a modern church centre in the rather more protestant part of Poland south of Katowice. On this trip I do not recall looking at a single bird. Several hundred students were joined by Christian workers, including some revived Roman Catholics, and maybe some who were not so revived but teaching theology and interested to see what those funny Protestants got up to. John engaged them all in discussion, often resorting to German when they could not cope with English.

Bill and Shirley Lees, formerly missionaries in Borneo, also shared in this conference and helped staff and students towards a wider vision of God's world. Poland, as most of Eastern Europe, was very cut off from missionary work and involvement in the days of communist domination. As the days of the strictest rule gradually eased, so more missionaries spread the vision. John Wallis, formerly with the Overseas Missionary Fellowship (O.M.F.) in Korea and Dick Dowsett, also previously working with O.M.F. in the Philippines, ministered at several different student camps. Gradually the seed was sown which has resulted in East European students now being called by God into mission work.

I shall always remember returning to Lausanne in 1971 for the first annual review of our work. I left with my heart absolutely singing. Stacey was such a great boss to work for. The only co-ordinating force for the whole of IFES was that illustrious man and here was I, a mere novice, reporting directly to him. Unfailingly direct and honest, he was always challenging and encouraging us to give of our best for the Lord's sake. We had looked back on the ways our good God had led us, saw how much we had accomplished, and all in safety! God had kept us.

We had travelled across many borders, visited many churches and students, alone or in little groups, but had not been incarcerated as I'm sure Stacey feared we would be and as some West German staff workers had been a year or so earlier. They suffered nightmares for years after their ordeal at the hands of the Stasi—arrest, questioning, being obliged to divulge information about the students they had gone hoping to encourage, the trial and the imprisonment which followed. Their mission to help their brothers in the East sadly backfired while ours got off to a flying start. We were beginning to kindle interest, light up the fires, and spread the flames of enthusiasm. We had benefited so much from meeting with fellow staff. We were not formally trained, but we were set good examples, and we learnt as we went along, God keeping us from making any disastrous mistakes. Of course we started on a wide front—the whole of Eastern Europe—and only later as the fire spread and movements were formally established did the rate of organisational change become ferocious. To begin with, while not exactly being cloak-and-dagger workers, we simply kept a low profile and were as unobtrusive as possible while constantly working to expand IFES's horizons in the East.

Of course, IFES had no political intentions or goals. Our aim was purely to help the Christian students to live out their lives in obedience to God's will, and we never saw that as incompatible with being good and honest citizens, even under a communist regime. But the secret police were naturally suspicious and constantly looking for money passing to buy influence or for any wrong motive. We had to take Jesus' words very seriously when he said to his disciples, "I am sending you out like sheep among wolves. Therefore be as shrewd as serpents and as innocent as doves." Matt 10:16. As we had to show constantly, and to all, how innocent we were, we found it much easier, and better, to say that we had called on the recommendation of a mutual friend! To begin with the mutual friend might have been Stacey Woods himself, or another of the small band of missionaries we gradually discovered were working in Eastern Europe.

We continually wrote reports back to Stacey, but it was our visits to Lausanne that I particularly remember. On these occasions Stacey would discuss our performance and the problems we were having with the job and he would challenge and encourage us to do better. This personal interaction was, I found, very beneficial. I had received no formal training for the job but what Stacey offered was almost like a one-to-one training course. What a privilege to be tutored by the great man! Gradually we probably did work more to his satisfaction. The one-year contract was renewed for another year, then for a further two and so on. Thus we worked on for 10 years, on the basis of meeting and encouraging students and church leaders personally because their friend so-and-so had suggested we should call to see them!

Later on we were asked a good question by another General Secretary of IFES. "Where does your support lay?"enquired Chua Wee Hian. The answer was that it lay, for the most part, exactly among those to whom we had been sent. These were the people who prayed for us, constantly. They knew the dangers we faced almost daily. These were the people who unstintingly gave us hospitality, sharing with us from their need, and sometimes even their poverty, their lodging and their meals. A Christian doctor in Romania gave me medicine when my stomach was badly upset with gastro-enteritis. A chemistry graduate in Hungary gave us a long tow when our car broke down in Budapest and we needed to get it to the right garage over the border in Austria to have it fixed. A graduate in Slovakia fixed the car when it was snowing and the car developed electrical problems. He was much more than a car mechanic, (he had a doctorate from Oxford) but was concerned in such a down-to-earth practical way for us. So loyal was he to his country that he had returned home from Oxford when requested to do so by his embassy. Then again I shall always remember the father of two students we visited in Sofia, Bulgaria, who filled our tank from a big can of petrol he produced, and wished us well for the journey with a "come again soon!"

IFES was run on a shoe-string, our operations too. We would never want to squander money which Christian believers had sacrificially given towards the work of extending the kingdom in the hearts and minds of students, so we always tried to make the money spin out as much as possible, and the Lord always saw to it that we had just enough to carry on. Just enough were the operative words. More than once we returned to our temporary base at Schloß Mittersill from a long journey—several weeks travelling around south-east Europe—our money all spent and, incredibly, the petrol indicator on zero too! We had so little disposable income that every penny really counted. At home in England our village pastor, Gordon Diamond, must have noticed how little we had because at Christmas he arranged for a box of goodies to be left for us, a gift from an unnamed mutual friend. When on the road, a fill of petrol, meals or a bed for the night in a friendly home were almost beyond price.

We did receive a modest salary, but needed to take every opportunity to make the money go further by our personal imports of gifts or purchases. Prices in those days were heavily subsidised in

Eastern Europe. As we were there anyway for the work we brought back our choice of useful souvenirs: jams from Yugoslavia, where we also bought our first barbecue and around which so many friends have since been regaled at our garden parties; bottled fruit, mostly cherries and plums, from Czechoslovakia; delicious limpid liquid gold acacia honey and tasty sausages from Hungary; hard yellow cheese; and cheap but cheerful and above all very practical notebooks from Poland or Romania. As a treat, we would bring back a small piece of smoked ham from East Germany or a box containing a real Dresdner stollen—a Christmas cake delicacy which could be bought cheaply in the supermarket in Dresden itself—in January when the price had been lowered!

It was also in my early years with IFES that I developed my enthusiasm for gardening. We had a small garden outside our cottage in Sussex in southern England, and we realised that it could be made to provide quantities of fruit and vegetables for us to enjoy and to give away—but also to help extend our finances. Have you ever worked in a garden? Like mission work it is a constant challenge though more relaxing for the mind. If you garden you will know that coping with the weeds is the number one priority. Weeds are like sin in our lives. Some are easier to eradicate than others, and bindweed is like persistent sin—awfully hard to deal with. Like some sin it even has a fancy name to give it respectability, Morning Glory. Now who could ever suspect Morning Glory of being the worst weed in the garden? Try to dig it up and the roots break and it splits itself into many plants to trouble you in the future. Ignore it at your peril. It creeps up all but unseen amongst the raspberries, and bursts into flower before you know where you are. Pull at it then and it is so tough that the delicate raspberry canes suffer more than the bindweed!

But gardening is a wonderful hobby too. We took plants as gifts to friends in Yugoslavia and Germany and Poland and in return we found we were blessed by other friendly gardeners. Even this year I have prayed for Peter and Jan who are members of our home church as often as I have enjoyed the autumn raspberries they so generously shared. Perhaps they will also pray for us when they enjoy red currants from the bush I shared with them. In another corner stands a pretty little tree given by the first lady, Mary Turvey, who noticed that Anikó was pregnant with David, over 30 years ago! I did not plant our pear tree (Williams pears, of course) but when it did not produce fruit a professional gardener suggested feeding it. Cultivate all good and beautiful things, just as the Apostle Paul exhorts. "You plant pears for your heirs", said the gardener

But perhaps my favourites are the Hungarian plum trees. These were sent back by my mother-in-law with Chris Davies, our colleague and friend, who flew to London from Budapest after a time there encouraging the emergent student movement. British Airways wrapped them up very grandly in a huge polythene bag. Chris thought she'd better declare them on arrival at Heathrow. She went into the red channel to declare, "I have brought these plum trees!" The customs officer looks up plum trees in his fat book of rules. "Are they annuals or perennials?" asks this inhabitant of London's concrete jungle. "I don't know." replied Chris who lived in the same concrete jungle. "You'd better go," says the customs man. They lived for at least 10 years so I took it that they turned out to be perennial plum trees. One of them bore around 50 pounds of delicious blue plums one autumn, ideal for plum dumplings!

POLISH PRELUDE

I doubt very much whether I would have ever been able to go abroad to Poland in the first place without the help of Dick Lucas, Rector of St Helen's Church, Bishopsgate, in London. How did this come about, especially as I was never a member of his congregation?

In the summer of 1962, soon after I was converted, I attended the IVF student camp at Keswick a little town which nestles below spectacular hills in the English Lake District. A large Christian convention is held there annually under marquees, which do their best to keep off copious falls of summer rain. I met a very fine Christian student from Trinity College, Cambridge at this camp. Frank Grenfell was also a new Christian, and we meant business when, in the marquee, we stood together in response to a challenge to be prepared to go anywhere and do anything to serve the Lord. On graduation, Frank went to Uganda—a more typical missionary field for Englishmen!

At Keswick, I did not have the slightest inkling that God would be calling me to serve him in Poland, and later with the IFES throughout Eastern Europe. But in God's good plan, another significant meeting turned out to be the camp open day. This was a fun occasion, when all sorts of interesting people were invited to have tea and talk to us students, before being 'entertained' in an appropriately Christian manner, by some singers and musicians. Major Bill Batt was camp commandant and I was his batman for this camp. I cleaned his shoes and ran his errands! At an evangelistic meeting in the town, Major Batt, good military man that he was, told the townsfolk of Keswick how he would love to march them all straight into the Kingdom of God. I rather fancy that it was Major Batt who introduced me to Dick Lucas. We chatted, and I gave Dick a cup of tea. English people do love their tea!

Two years were to pass before I was to meet Dick again, also over tea. This time, I was in my final year at Leeds University. After graduation, I was hoping to take up a Polish Government Scholarship to attend the Academy of Mining and Metallurgy in Cracow to do a postgraduate apprenticeship. I did not think there was anything particularly odd about this although it would have been far from first choice for many other students. 20 or so postgraduate scholarships were open for British graduates to apply for. I had already spent a happy vacation in Poland, arranged for me by my good Polish friend Mirosław Grylicki who I knew from his time in Leeds. I was based at the Refractories Institute in Gliwice where he usually worked. I was also sponsored for the vacation study by a little organisation with a grand title—The International Association for the Exchange of Students for Technical Experience, (known to the initiated as IAESTE). So my Polish Government Scholarship seemed just the right way forward.

Dick Lucas appeared in the middle of a Sunday afternoon foreign students tea party I attended at St. George's vicarage in Leeds. Mary Turvey, the vicar's wife, was passing round tea, scones and sandwiches, and the foreign students were there to be welcomed and to swell the evening congregation. Raymond, Mary's husband, brought Dick into the room where this very English cultural performance was going on. Dick looked round at the assembled company, and, looking at me, said: "I know you, don't I?" From there on we chatted. Dick asked me about my studies and what I had in mind to do after graduating. If I had been training for the ordained ministry I would not have been going to Poland. If I had already been trained as a missionary, I would not have been going to Poland—Poland did not welcome foreign missionaries in 1966! But as a 'tentmaker', as a research worker in ceramics, I was welcome.

There was only one cloud on the horizon: my parents were dead against my going. After meeting Dick again, I wrote to my father, who was working in London and had started to go to St Helen's on Tuesdays for their lunchtime services. I said that we had had Dick Lucas visit us at Leeds over the weekend. "Oh, I know all about that" he replied. On the Monday, Dick had returned to London and had a special lunchtime meeting to tell his congregation about a trip he had just made to the United States before coming to Leeds. How did I come in to a de-briefing on the US? That I may never know, but my father was there in St Helen's, and without Dick mentioning my name he recognised who Dick was talking about. My parents' opposition to my accepting the Polish scholarship vanished at that point! In fact, my father had excellent connections with the merchant navy where he had worked his way up to the rank of captain. He actually fixed me up with a very reasonably priced ticket for my two-and-a-half day sea passage from London to Gdynia, Poland's main Baltic port.

After a night ashore, an early morning train carried me to Warsaw to make the acquaintance of certain Christian contacts of Dr John Laird, then General Secretary of Scripture Union in London. Dr Laird had not long since been on a missionary journey to Poland, with the aim of extending Scripture Union's outreach there. How would I ever have managed without his contacts and his kind letters of introduction? Certainly, I'd have had a much slower start and many more difficulties.

As it was, by the time the overnight train carried me onwards from Warsaw across Poland to Cracow, I had had the good fortune to meet Aleksander Kircun senior. People told me he had single-handedly started up the Baptist church in Warsaw again after the Second World War. He had also given his daughter, Ludmiła, to be the wife of Krzysztof Bednarczyk. Having had a letter of introduction from Dr. Laird to Aleksander Kircun in Warsaw, I now had a letter of introduction to Krzysztof, then pastor of the Baptist congregation. As I was to find out quite soon he was the only one of all the pastors of Protestant Churches in Cracow who could speak English!

Had God not prepared and led me in his way for me? Through his kindness and love he called me, he opened the door and he showed me the way he had prepared for me to follow him, to serve him, and to find wonderful peace and satisfaction in doing so.

Through the Bednarczyks I met my dear wife, and for a time not only did Anikó travel with me after I joined the IFES, but also acted as my secretary. Then, as the children began to make increasing demands on her time, she was able to do less and less secretarial work, let alone travelling. Sir Fred Catherwood, treasurer of the IFES, took pity on me at this point, and early in 1976 a new secretary arrived. The marvellous and multi-talented Liz Paisley is an amazing person. Even with no understanding of the Polish language she was quite capable of typing a letter in Polish. She organised me and greatly strengthened the work at this time, writing my letters and reports, and enabling us to publish Bible study guides in Polish and Hungarian, which was an enormous assistance for the small student groups getting going at that time.

We did not stop at letters and reports. Liz also beavered away at Ada Lum's "Responsible Evangelism"—the why and how of reaching your friends through small evangelistic Bible studies. The Polish "Responsible Evangelism", like the Hungarian version, was produced 100 or so at a time, duplicated and delivered personally to the students. Ada Lum was a very generous, if unusual, author. Censorship meant her books would never have arrived if sent through the post. We likewise produced small editions of evangelistic Bible studies for small group use and we published hymn books in different languages, for use at Mittersill and then back home for the Polish and Hungarian Christian student groups.

Sir Fred and Lady Elizabeth Catherwood were welcoming and generous houseparents at the summer student camp in Mittersill in 1976. They threw a tea-party for us and all the students from Eastern Europe on the terrace by the summer-house with its intricately decorated green tiled stove. I never knew this stove to ever be heated, but it was a thing of great craft and beauty. Over tea the Catherwoods spoke with each of "our" students including one of the few students able to come from Romania at that time. He was Abel Tan a fine young and nimble Christian Filipino man we had met as a foreign student in Timişoara. Abel had Christian friends in England, people he had known in the Phillipines, and who he wished to visit before returning home from Europe. Abel had his return air ticket. He had been to Bucharest for a British visa. We offered to bring him back to England, and Sir Fred kindly said that, should we have difficulties with immigration we were to phone him. He was President of the Board of Trade at that time, and knew the British Home Secretary (Interior Minister) personally. We knew that U.K. immigration could be difficult, so, leaving Mittersill, we called in at the British Consulate in Innsbruck along our way. The Consul assured us that Abel's visa was in order, but that the final decision always rested with the immigration officer at the port of entry. He told us of people who had been turned back despite their visas being in order. We did not tell him that we had Sir Fred's phone number!

At Dover the following evening, sure enough we did have a grilling from immigration. Abel was taken off to be interviewed, and we were interviewed separately. How did we know Abel? Was he not just a hitch-hiker we had picked up somewhere? Later Abel told us that the immigration officer had been asking many very personal questions which he found highly embarrassing. How did he know the people he was intending to visit? Who was his girl friend? Was he not planning to stay in the U.K. and marry? After a good hour of interviews and waiting I asked the officer we were with if the end was now in sight. "No, it isn't," he replied. "So may I use the phone?" I queried. A short call to Sir Fred, who had flown home to London while we were travelling over land, and the end came quicker than either immigration or I had believed possible. Abel stayed with us in Sussex for a few days, memorably climbing a tree in our garden to prune a few branches, visited his friends in London and quietly departed for Romania.

Ada Lum was a frequent teacher at our summer student training camps, enthusiastically telling the students how easy it was for them to gather a few friends over a cup of coffee in a café or dormitory, almost anywhere in fact. She would tell them how to discuss topics from the Bible, so that Jesus would come alive in everyday situations. Students would quickly see how relevant Jesus could be—"Jesus Against the Capitalists" (John 2:13-25), "Jesus Talks with Leaders of Society" (John 3:1-13), "Jesus Breaks the Barriers of Tradition" (John 4:1-30).

John Stott too taught the students through Bible expositions at certain conferences, at Oak Hill Theological College in the summer of 1977, and at the IFES European Easter Conference on Evangelism in Würzburg, Germany, in 1988. Anikó did simultaneous interpretation for him on both these occasions, and at Würzburg first recorded her interpretation for wider distribution. His visits to the different East European countries were valuable in themselves, but his writings were a vital and longer lasting part of our armoury in encouraging and building up the students in their faith. I recall visiting a student in Prague. On his bookshelf I was thrilled to find not only a Bible but also a copy of John Stott's "Basic Christianity". Anikó used both the Polish and German versions of Basic Christianity as well as the English original when preparing her Hungarian translation. It was then published by Harmat in Budapest. The Hungarian Literature Mission, based in Stuttgart, bound Anikó's translation of John Stott's "Being a Christian" with "Invitation to Live", which was published separately in English by Scripture Union. These translations wonderfully extended John's ministry among students and many other people in many countries. Some theological students also used two chapters of Stott's "Our Guilty Silence" which Anikó worked on for the Theological Education by Extension team based in Vienna, (also known as Bible Education by Extension). Another significant publication was the Hungarian edition of John's "Baptism and Fullness" which Anikó translated and for which he graciously wrote a special new foreword. I have listed only the works by John Stott which Anikó translated, but amongst other material she has also worked on a commentary of the whole Bible and a three-year course of Bible reading notes for children and families, which Scripture Union have published in Hungary.

Early on during my days in Cracow, Dr Laird of Scripture Union came out from England and participated in a special evangelistic Inter-Church week among the non-Roman Catholic Churches in Warsaw. A feature of this week was the exchange of pulpits among the churches for evening services. So, for example, a priest from the Orthodox church in Warsaw spoke one evening in the Warsaw Baptist church on the text "Come unto me all you who are heavy laden, and I will give you rest. Take my yoke upon you, and learn of me..". It was very moving for me as an evangelical Englishman to hear the words of Jesus—the Gospel, the Good News of salvation, from the lips of an Orthodox priest!

The Orthodox are an amazing part of the Christian Church. Superficially, with their churches richly decorated with icons and swinging incense during their services, they look very much like Roman Catholics, but when you get to know people with an Orthodox faith, you discover that some are often very keen on studying the Bible and have a deep love for the Lord. I had not met such folk before, and this was a surprise to me. Officially there is often not much co-operation between Orthodox and Evangelicals, just as suspicion tends to exist between Roman Catholics and Evangelicals, but on an individual level, at the grass roots, there can be a surprising working together for the same goal, to draw people closer to the Lord Jesus through his Word.

It is not part of Orthodox theology that Romanians, Russians, Serbs or Ukrainians can only be Orthodox, but there is a great deal of religious nationalism which largely dictates that this is so, just as it has been for centuries. On the other hand, Poles and Croats tend to be very nationalistic Roman Catholics, and their priests can be dead set against anything the Evangelicals dare or care to do. So it was truly amazing and unusual that, during the earlier parts of the days of that week in Warsaw, the leaders of the various churches could meet in solemn council to discuss the evangelisation of Poland. They may not actually have arrived at a grand strategy, but the meetings certainly served to promote friendly co-operation and mutual understanding.

Soon Krzysztof Bednarczyk was travelling to the Soviet Union with an ecumenical party, on an official visit to the Russian

Orthodox Church. They knew that as official visitors they would be whisked through customs, so they were almost all very well stocked up with Russian Bibles. Those were the days when Bibles were in very short supply in Russia, and when the Soviet customs were keen to spot and confiscate any they could—but not from such official visitors! Then we had an exchange of pulpits in Cracow. There was not such a variety in the non-Catholic Churches, but a particularly memorable event was Krzysztof taking a party of students to the Benedictine priory at Tyniec, a few kilometres west of Cracow on a high bank above the River Vistula (Wisła). There we discussed with the Benedictine monks how we had each become a Christian!

These Benedictines were giving religious instruction to some of the local children, and for comparison wanted to get to know how we had come in our different ways to a living faith in the Lord Jesus Christ. Soon it was time for lunch. We were honoured to be invited to join them for a simple meal of boiled fish and potatoes served at long, bare, scrubbed wooden refectory tables. The meal was taken in silence, apart from one Brother who stood in a corner of the refectory and read to us from the then very newly translated and published Thousand Year Bible (Bibia Tysiąc Lecia), which was the first major new Polish Bible translation for four hundred years. Much of the translation work had been done there at Tyniec by the very monks who were entertaining us.

Dr Laird had had great success at the discussion of evangelism in Warsaw. Many of the Churches decided to take a considerably larger number of the daily Bible reading calendars which Scripture Union had already been publishing. The Orthodox Church became the largest subscriber, with over 2,000 calendars. The Lutherans, Methodists, and United Evangelical Church joined the Baptists, to swell the number of Poles taking those little cards to over 20,000 each year. Many copies were treasured and re-used in some difficult years when supplies did not arrive because they were confiscated at customs or later when Scripture Union tried to print in Poland, but ran into technical difficulties (the Poles honestly thought Scripture Union in England had run out of paper!)

The Roman Catholics never did subscribe formally to this Bible reading plan. However many individual Catholics received copies from friends and the little cards proved excellent to give to students and young people who were either newly converted or just interested in Christianity. They had, in addition to a Bible reading plan, a simple guide instructing readers how to pray, and urging them not to do either read or pray mechanically. A few questions they could ask about any Bible passage were also listed to stimulate thought and prayer. These guides also gave the encouragement, very valuable for Poles cut off behind the Iron Curtain, that everyone who used these calendars was joining many thousands of others worldwide. The new translations—the Thousand Year Bible being soon joined by a new Protestant Bible Society edition—meant the ground was already being laid for a great harvest of people whom God would be bringing to faith in Christ over the next decade.

Scripture Union has gone from strength to strength, in Poland and in different ways in every East European country. David Blair, who in 1996 led, co-ordinated and was midwife to the emerging Scripture Union movements, first travelled to Eastern Europe almost 20 years earlier, when he was seconded to join me for a children's camp in Bielice to train leaders. A high school girl, Niusia Zachanowicz, wanted to organise a Bible camp for her school friends and teachers and was asking for help.

Who could have foreseen the significance back then of taking David along? We travelled by car through Germany and Czechoslovakia, arriving in time to spend the night in Plzeň, famous for its Pilsner lager. Had the troops in the Soviet Army convoy been consuming this beverage before taking to the road? We passed part of a long troop convoy but due to the rather narrow winding road were caught behind yet another truck of Russian soldiers. They couldn't ask their driver in the front cab for a comfort stop and didn't seem to mind us watching them making themselves more comfortable out of the back of the truck!

We arrived in Plzeň after dark. It was as gloomy as most towns in Eastern Europe were. We had booked a hotel but did not know exactly where it was. In the West, such places are normally lit up with neon signs but not at this time in the East. "Where is the hotel?" I asked a local. "It's that barrack over there" he replied. Sure enough, it loomed up out of the dark, and although it was unlit by any bright advertising was quite adequate and clean, with both hot and cold running water.

Not all the leaders arrived in Bielice in time to be trained before that children's camp. Leaders were not used to being trained in those days and, anyway, Poland was the sort of laid-back place where the enthusiastic campers often arrived first, and then the leaders came, and only then would the camp eventually get going. We nevertheless had an excellent camp, inspiring for many older children and younger students and the leaders did learn on the job. Meanwhile, David Blair was getting a taste for the Lord's work in Eastern Europe, which would later involve him full-time for eight years. Gradually he found suitable staff and committee members and nurtured new Scripture Union movements into independent life across the whole area.

I recall at an early camp in Bielice, how David had been giving lectures on the influences which affect our Christian lives. After David left, Tomek Błażowski, then a physical education student in Katowice, continued with talks on other influences. Tomek was an expert skier, and very athletic, so the influences he mentioned were quite different from David's, with a different cultural perspective. Later Tomek became a Baptist pastor (and part-time ski instructor) at the ski resort of Wisła, and in 1996 joined the staff of Scripture Union in Poland.

Schoolchildren were seeing their class mates coming to the Lord. There was often a ripple effect. At one camp, we had a teacher with her husband, at another a headmaster with his wife and small daughter. We used to gather gifts from churches in England before setting off for these camps, as many items which we took for granted were unavailable in Poland. Sometimes it was soap, washing powder or even toilet paper, but mostly food items—those which do not grow in Poland. Students still remember the excitement of the aroma of coffee being made, in the days when it was an unbelievable luxury. I called in at the market in Brighton to purchase a box of lemons, which the Poles love to slice and add to their tea. Spices, which would liven up a cake or two, dried fruit which would also go into cakes or desserts, even a couple of huge pineapples on one memorable occasion. We offered the headmaster's daughter an orange, but she refused. She was three or four at the time and was frightened. She had never before seen an orange!

Did these camps do any good? It certainly seems they did. What a privilege I have had to be in this work long enough to see some of the ways God has led people on. The first step of coming to faith in him at an evangelistic camp often led to serving him and his Church in Christian and in secular life, and across the whole of Eastern Europe, in the vastly different and changed circumstances of today.

The main object of the camps in Poland was always to allow God to bless the Poles. He didn't stop there. Many visitors have also had their lives enriched through student camps in Poland. John Wallis, at the time Home Secretary of the Overseas Missionary Fellowship in England, offered to return many times after his first visit when we struggled through the city of Wrocław, strike-bound by Solidarity, and God amazingly provided lifts for us all the way to the front door of the house in Bielice 80 km away. John Wallis is a rather large man, and the most popular car in Poland at the time was the Polish Fiat 500, the smallest car imaginable. Would there be room for us both, not to mention our luggage? Our luggage sat on our knees, and amazingly we squeezed into the back of this 'shoe-box' sized vehicle.

Paul Markby came up to me after an evening service in our church quite a few years ago, and asked if he could join me on a camp at Bielice. I hesitated, not because he was a first-year student himself at the time, but because of the added responsibility I felt towards him as his father Peter was then our pastor. It certainly would not do for the pastor's son to break his leg in a fall on the ice in Poland! Many other members of our congregation at Southover, Lewes in Sussex have followed to various camps, and Paul himself has been back to Poland many times, including a summer school at the university in Cracow in the course of his studies in international relations.

I lived with my parents in Lindfield before I studied at Leeds, and even tried to teach in the Sunday School at All Saints, the parish church there, before I came to personal faith in Christ myself. Derek Heath, a patent agent, now a European Patent Attorney, also at that time from All Saints church in Lindfield, has enjoyed ministering at many camps for young people in Bielice and contributed substantially to the work of the English Language School in Wrocław. The first time Derek had a frightening adventure when he flew in an ancient rattletrap Tupolev aeroplane which shuddered into the air run by LOT, the Polish airline, to Warsaw and on to Wrocław. Derek's son Jeremy, about 20, bravely drove the family car laden with the dried fruit, oranges, toilet paper and other provisions hard to come by in Poland as well as Paul Markby and myself all across Europe for the camp. Derek was appalled at the way the Poles lived, commonly waiting for 20 years for a small flat, and then having to make do with accommodation designed for two people being used by three generations. Did the overcrowding contribute to the high divorce rate? The blocks of flats built under communism were usually grim, grey and poorly constructed from factory made concrete modules. These elements did hold together, but usually left unintentional gaps for the cold wind to whistle through. It was a shock for a comparatively affluent westerner to encounter such conditions. More solid were the pre-1939 flats—though by the 1980's these seemed to have particularly ancient plumbing which could creak and thud and a maze of pipes which had to be seen to be believed. Derek thought the conditions were Dickensian. Under communism in the mid 20th century if you belonged to the Party you enjoyed good housing, foreign holidays and medicines imported from the West. In fact you would live much like ordinary people in Western Europe. But most of the workers who supported the communist regime fared far worse. They experienced poor housing, tremendous difficulties in obtaining passports, no access to foreign currency to buy imported medicines, and inordinate difficulties in gaining a place to study at university.

Another noted author and speaker, Robert Parsons of the Christian charitable organisation 'Care for the Family', also contributed much, by way of inspiring lectures, as well as the loan of various cars in which, over recent years, I have transported a great many Polish and British volunteers as well as quantities of relief materials to Poland.

I think of another early camp, held in the large rooms of a Lutheran minister's 17th century vicarage. I was joined by David Blair, and Janusz Niwiński, a drummer in a dance band. Janusz had already been converted through a chance meeting on a bus with Gustaw Muszkiet, the warden at Bielice, who took him home and led him to a real, living faith in the Lord. Previously Janusz had been disillusioned with the formality of religious traditions, which was all he had known in the Roman Catholic Church. Janusz later studied for the ministry, while working in a Wrocław furniture factory to support himself and his young wife, Goscia. They were then sent out as missionaries to Szczytno, in north-east Poland, a needy town of some 32,000 with a tiny handful of believers scattered across the town and the surrounding countryside. Then there was Robert Miksa, who grew as a student leader and now pastors a large church in Gdańsk, and his church secretary, Ania Hryciuk, who arrived at a student camp as a very shy, quiet girl, and later blossomed through a Bible course with the organisation known as Torchbearers in England.

One of the privileges of being on the staff of the IFES was the wealth of excellent co-workers who could be called upon to add a little spice and variety to the ministry at various camps. On at least one occasion, I was joined by Noor van Haaften, who did sterling work getting the IFES affiliated student work (the ÖSM) on to its feet in Austria. In those days, Noor strummed her guitar. These days she works at home in Holland, producing programmes for the Dutch Christian radio and television station, EO.

On another memorable occasion, during February 1975, I was bound for an evangelistic camp at Bielice in Poland with David Burt, student worker and songwriter in Barcelona. For some reason, the people in Poland thought that a visitor from Spain was just about too good to be true. No Spaniard from Franco's fascist regime would be issued with a visa to visit the People's Republic of (Socialist) Poland, but David Burt travelled on a British passport—he just worked in Spain!

En route to this student ski camp in the mountains, David and I were due to pass through the city of Wrocław to inform Christian leaders there about what the Lord was doing in far off Spain. An evening meeting had been set up and leaders from the Protestant denominations invited. In God's goodness, we never arrived. Who spilt the beans, willingly or even unwittingly, to the Polish secret police we never knew but their representative, uninvited, was in attendance. David and I were in the car struggling through deep snow, ice and fog in Czechoslovakia, and reached Wrocław an hour or so after the meeting should have ended. So God spared us the interest of the secret police, both in the city and at our main event, the student camp.

We were often very conscious of God's good hand on us, protecting us. How many times the UB (Polish secret police) called on the leaders of the student work! They could not understand the foreign visitors and expected to find money changing hands and currency laws being broken. Sometimes we did have gifts of cash to take to help the building work in Bielice by paying for materials but we were careful never to infringe the regulations.

The Polish students themselves contributed the lion's share of the labour to convert the disused farm building at Bielice; they gave much of the finance too. The German Chairman of IFES, Dr Bodo Volkmann, arranged for a party of Polish students to spend a summer holiday working in Germany for the very purpose of raising the needed money. The UB would ask students to report back after visits abroad. They had to agree to do this before they would be issued with their passports. So visits to Germany for vacation work, or to Austria for Bible conferences at Mittersill really had to include a home visit to a real local family. The family would also have to be at home to entertain their student visitor at the very time when 99% of such families with children take their own holidays.

Again, we needed great wisdom in knowing when to associate ourselves with students at such public events as evangelistic camps, when others besides the trusted Christian students would be present. This was quite different from making home or individual visits. There was always the danger of foreigners being accused of something political against the state and of the student organisers of the event being accused as well, and subsequently losing their university place.

If we were reasonably careful, even as foreigners we could generally take part in student camps in Poland but that would have been too risky and seemed unwise throughout most of the communist period in Czechoslovakia. The Czech security service were considerably harder on their larger Protestant Churches than the Poles were on their comparatively smaller evangelical church communities. The most we could hope for in Czechoslovakia was an extended family holiday camp. Later, Czech students would come over into Poland to join in international student camps. It was probably easier for us in IFES for Czechs and Slovaks to travel to Austria. We took care only to invite Christian students whom we could trust but it was never easy. It was always stressful for them, both making application for their passports and again when going home and facing the secret service interview when they handed their passports back. Eventually, as conditions eased, camps proved possible also in Hungary—out in the remote countryside—but similar locations in Bulgaria or Romania would have been too risky for all concerned.

Thanks to inspiring international visiting speakers, and very ordinary foreign students, the Poles have often been reminded that the Christian world outside cared and had not forgotten them in their hard times and their struggles. This meant a lot to them, and they would often tell us so especially during those years when they found it almost impossible to travel abroad. Visiting them at home in Poland was, in comparison, often much less risky.

Just occasionally some brave soul would kick up a fuss about being refused permission to travel. When Franciszek Blachnicki was refused a passport for a visit to the West in 1980, he responded with an open letter written to the Polish Minister of Internal Affairs.[19]

"Since the very inception of the present political system of the Polish People's Republic, the passport policy of the security police has been an instrument for the limitation of freedom, the discrimina-

tion, vexation and blackmail of citizens, and the violation and deprivation of conscience.

In every state of the world with a democratic system the permanent possession of a passport is an expression of citizen's rights, viewed in the same way as the possession of a personal identity card. In Poland, on the other hand, receiving of a passport is an act of grace on the part of the security police. No one knows what must be done to merit it, and when one does one feels as though one had been released from prison. In the company of people from free, democratic states, we must constantly appear as slaves, answering invitations to take part in various meetings with: 'I don't know whether I will receive a passport, or whether I will receive one in time, or whether they will let me go.' That is to say nothing of the fact that even when we finally 'succeed' in travelling abroad, we must then appear to the world as beggars, unable to support ourselves with our own Polish money."

He continued: *"Since the situation described above, which results from the present passport law and the policies of the security police, amount to the restriction of freedom, and thus a form of imprisonment, you will find enclosed with this document my personal identity card (No. ZN 1988677), which I am relinquishing to the Ministry of Internal Affairs. After all, prisoners do not carry their personal identity documents with them, but must surrender them to the prison authorities. I do not desire to maintain the illusion, created by carrying a personal identity card, that I am a free person when in fact this freedom is denied me.*

"I would also like to contribute in this way to the acceleration of the process of authentic democratisation and national liberation. Among other things, this process must include a change in the passport law, giving citizens permanent passports and the right to cross the border at any time, as long as there is no legitimate cause properly verified by due process of law, to restrict this freedom for the common good."

Faced with such an open letter the authorities caved in and Blachnicki was granted his passport, though it was still going to be another eight years before Poles would be able to keep their passports at home and 'cross the border at any time'.

More recently groups of young people and students from St Helen's Church in London have given and received much, as they have worked and helped on numerous evangelistic camps at Bielice. Of course, willing hands are useful in the kitchen. Camp vegetables do not come out of tins in Poland—all need to be cleaned and peeled. They took part in digging foundations out of the solid rock. In one camp we saw the walls rise and the roof go on too. Above all, they made friends with the Poles, getting alongside them at a football match or on excursions, and teaching English in small groups where everyone was included. Every Christian visitor had the opportunity to share in a relaxed way, day after day, from the Bible as an English teaching tool and from their own personal walk of faith. So friendships have been formed, and faith shared. In such ways the kingdom of God is still being built today among the students of capitalist Poland, just as it was among those of socialist Poland in years now past.

POLISH PROGRESS

I have to thank Professor Nadachowski, my mentor during a two year postgraduate apprenticeship in the Department of Refractory Materials at the Academy of Mining and Metallurgy, Cracow, in Poland (1966—1968) for his wise counsel and advice—particularly in times of political tension.

Polish workers went on strike in the spring of 1967, and the students supported them by gathering to demonstrate in large numbers. Thousands filled the main Cracow city square. One dear Christian man from the Cracow Baptist church, a kind husband and the father of two teenagers in the church, worked in the famous 'Lenin' steel mill at Nowa Huta, 10 km to the east of Cracow. He was so seriously wounded by blows from the police during a demonstration that he needed treatment in hospital! The pastor, the Reverend Krzysztof Bednarczyk, visited him in the hospital and was shaken to see him in such a state.

The early demonstrations had been peaceful marches, with some of those at the front carrying placards. At that time, the police had not received orders to crack down, so they just kept the traffic away and made sure the demonstration was peaceful. The next day was quite a different story. Orders had come through, and the police were out in force, wielding their batons. We were lucky they did not have orders to shoot.

The same happened in Gliwice, where I was going regularly for my scientific studies. The large Silesian Polytechnic is based in Gliwice and students massed in their thousands outside the main building in the vast square normally used only for such official events as communist military parades and May 1st political rallies. The students moved silently towards the statue of Adam Mickiewicz, the Polish 'Shakespeare' whose statue stands in many Polish towns including Cracow's famous market square.

The Soviet Ambassador to Poland was severely displeased with anti-Russian sentiments in one of Mickiewicz's plays, staged in Warsaw, and insisted that this production, though passed by the Polish Government censor, be withdrawn at once. This high-handed action, demonstrating less cautiously than usual who was really in charge in Warsaw, incensed ordinary workers all over Poland—nowhere less than in Nowa Huta, which was making steel almost entirely for export to the Soviet Union at a very nominal price. But the price to the Polish environment, and in particular to the mediaeval stonework of the city of Cracow as well as to the Niepołomice forest outside the city, was not at all nominal.

The students were ready to support the workers and also had their own grievances. Almost everyone hated being obliged to study political economy which preached the inevitable triumph of communism/state socialism over the corrupt and depraved world of capitalism. Meanwhile much material, particularly historical, was locked away, unavailable to anyone.

Not all Christians saw the issue in such black and white terms. I was criticised by a Christian professor for supporting the demonstrations, but my own Professor Nadachowski just told me to keep my head down, and: "Make sure you always have a cup of coffee or a glass of wine on offer when you have friends round to your college room for a Bible study". How, I wondered, did he know about those Bible study sessions I was having with various students? That was a mystery. The surveillance system was obviously working, yet it was still OK for me to continue. I must have been seen at the demonstrations too.

I started evangelistic Bible studies in my college room in English when I first arrived. My student friends had no choice but to speak to me in English. But by my second year, my Polish improved to such an extent that we changed over to Polish evangelistic Bible studies, and I could invite any or all of my ever-widening circle of friends. Which of them was working for the UB, (the Urząd Bezpieczeństwa—Security Service or Secret Police) I will never know. Years later, I am still good friends with several of them. One, a Catholic Christian, teaches English at the Jagiellonian University in Cracow. Another, who was studying engineering at the time, was soundly converted through a visit to an early student camp run by the IFES at Mittersill. He grew as a Christian when he visited the United States, and currently teaches English while working with the Church of Free Christians (Brethren).

Dr. Mirosław Grylicki was my very first Polish friend, from the time when he arrived on a United Nations Scholarship at Leeds University where I was an undergraduate, and 'Ceramics Alex' duly met him on the platform as his train pulled in. Looking back now, I see the good hand of God arranging that UN scholarship. Even so, my training did not take place so much in the laboratories of the Institute of Refractory Materials as in the student residence.

The first time I went to Gliwice, as an undergraduate in 1965, I was accommodated in a student house at the far end of Ulica Pszczyńska. It was tough arriving back at the railway station late at night, and I could not get a taxi home! Taxis were very reasonable, especially for foreigners—even foreign students—but no way could I get my tongue round 'Pszczyńska'. To say this word, you need to almost sneeze in the middle of it. (My Polish has improved now, so I sneeze in the right place to order!) This road, Ulica Pszczyńska, leads to the pretty little country town of Pszczyna with its fine old mansion, (dwór in Polish, like the Russian dacha), surrounded with a fine well-wooded park, in which roams a herd of bison. To be faced with such a linguistic hurdle on my first visit to Poland was really tough. I'm only glad I didn't live in Warsaw on Aleja Krakowskie Przedmieście (Avenue to the Environs of Cracow). Words like these make Polish sound as though the speaker has drunk an excess of fizzy soda water which is now gushing out.

Based in Cracow for my studies my need grew for a spell in Gliwice. Not only were the laboratory facilities better there but so was the food. I was in my second year in Poland now, and, for some reason I never discovered, my entitlement to eat in the Cracow student canteen had been for one year only. This Cracow canteen was presided over by its resident manager, Pan Żołądek, amazingly Mr Stomach. He would stand, with his hands clasped under it, beaming a satisfying well-fed sort of smile at the queuing students. Whoever said not to trust a thin cook would have heartily approved of Pan Żołądek!

In my second year I tried cooking for myself but without a kitchen it was difficult. But I did manage roast hare and one fine Christmas pudding, cooked in the kiln in my laboratory. Shopping was also a major problem. Queuing for every item (the supermarket had hardly arrived in Poland in those days) simply took up too much time. A friend suggested I try a private restaurant. These were in people's homes, where a housewife would cook for around a dozen people each week-day. Though not as expensive as the public restaurants, they were too expensive to use regularly on a Polish Government Scholarship of 1,400 złoty (at that time #100 U.S.$) per month. I would have had no money left for travel, let alone buying items for my 'bottom drawer'.

Gliwice was God's complete answer to all my problems. During an IFES summer camp at Casa Moscia in Switzerland, I met Jan Wojnar, who was a student at Gliwice. There were three bunk beds in his room there and he was sharing the room with one other student, who apparently did little studying and was, in fact, away making money on private export/import business most of the time.

Private enterprise was not officially encouraged at that time but that did not stop quite a number of Poles from making a living as primitive capitalists, just by travelling with a couple of suitcases. They bought items in Poland they could sell at a better price in Czechoslovakia; in Czechoslovakia they bought goods they could sell for a profit in Hungary and so on throughout the communist block. Profits from such private business were sufficient to cover travel and accommodation and leave a little at the end of the trip. After a while you simply did not need to study to get a 'proper job'!

Jan Wojnar arranged for me to share his room in Gliwice and soon I was meeting all his Christian friends too. Here was an embryonic Christian Union! We regularly studied the Bible together and had an occasional 'agape'—a 'love feast' meal, with music played and sung by Jan and his friends, to which many other students came. These students didn't always wait to be invited to a properly organised 'agape'. One evening, a music practice session was in progress in Jan's room. Jan was on the 'cello and others were on the violin and flute, when a fellow arrived through the open window! Considering we lived on the second floor, this was quite a surprise. He heard the music, and, wanting to find us, crept along the narrow ledge outside the building. We were glad that God saved him from falling off—and later went on to save him for eternity.

Jan is now the successful director of a business called 'Sunny', which trades in Belarus, the Czech Republic and Poland. He told me recently about a man who called to see him saying he represented a Polish firm looking for offices to rent. "Because I wasn't using all my space at the time I was glad to talk with him." Jan told me. "I wanted to know what sort of person this potential renter was. My guest turned out to be the amiable director of a firm from Bielsko-Biała. After the arrangements had been made, we said farewell, and I gave him my business card so we could keep in touch. Then the real talking started. Looking at my name he slapped his forehead and sat down in a state of shock. "I actually know you," he exclaimed, admitting that he used to work at the local branch of the State Security Office where my name was widely known. What he went on to say really surprised me. "Now I understand! You never did behave as an ordinary fellow. It has all come back to me as in a film, and I just felt as though I was going through all those Security Office meetings again with the Security men." (They used to behave as if they ruled the world.) "I couldn't even think then that my situation would change so much, but the way you behaved then led me to change my whole world view." Not only had the State Security been in charge of passports, they had also been pressurising Jan to report back on what he and others did when he went abroad to IFES student conferences. "We know all about you, and what you do", they would boast. Even if not true, it was part of the pressure under which almost all active Christians lived under socialism. State Security officers searched Jan's flat for contraband on one occasion; they had an arrest warrant when they arrived but had found nothing they could charge Jan with. Neither had Jan betrayed IFES or its links—and now this former official respected him for his upright life.

Jan also told me about his first IFES meeting. "I had been invited to a Bible course in Switzerland. I had to ask several times before I was granted a passport, and then, for the first time in my life I crossed the border out of communism. It was overwhelming for me to meet so many Christian students from all over Europe and to hear the lectures given by IFES staff in Casa Moscia. People from Eastern Europe were not well understood in the free West, but simply to be invited convinced us of the great power of the Gospel. Contact with IFES became the inspiration for organising similar meetings in our country. Later I was to visit Mittersill, and there I first spoke to my future wife. We have four children, whom we trust will also grow to maturity in the Lord. All thanks to the fact that someone, one day, thought about a poor student from Poland and invested some money and time and all that was needed to bring us to listen to God's Word."

"Poland in 1995 is a completely different country to that of fifteen or even five years ago," writes Ewa Barciszewska, then a Polish student and now a journalist. "The change in the country's organisation and structure has brought a lot of good, though at the same time many bad things. It is a wonderful feeling to be able to take my passport out of the drawer at any time and go somewhere. It is also great that I can write about anything without fear of censorship, and I can read and become acquainted with different opinions, positions and world outlooks. It is a pleasure to see the shops full of goods, so you don't have to stand in a monstrous queue to buy a single item. But money is required too. No doubt 15 years ago, there was poverty in Poland. I saw degenerates or alcoholics then but hardly any beggars. At that time I hardly ever saw older, modestly dressed people, searching for something in rubbish bins or buying a single

slice of cheese and a roll. Old age was dignified then. Today the thought of growing old horrifies me. I am simply afraid that I will find myself without the means of support in my old age. My current earnings do not permit me to save for my old age."

I mentioned buying things for my 'bottom drawer'. This is the expression we use for articles we gather together in anticipation of setting up a new home. Yes, I got engaged to be married to Anikó. I met her off the Budapest-to-Warsaw express in Katowice and popped the question in a first class carriage during the journey from Katowice to Cracow. There was only one spare seat in the compartment but the other passengers did not seem to mind the two of us squeezing into one first-class seat. I wonder if they realised the serious nature of the conversation we were having!

Most of our courtship was conducted by post between Cracow and Budapest but we did have some precious times together in the winter of '67, in Cracow with its exceptionally fine museums and art galleries, Friday and Saturday evening orchestral concerts, exhibitions (I recall a magnificent one of art and artifacts from China) and varied cultural life. One day we took two of the Bednarczyk children to the famous salt mines, at Wieliczka just outside Cracow. You can see how rock salt was mined in the middle ages. Not only mined, but also carved, into chandeliers, figures and statues of Mary and Jesus to grace ancient chapels set up in excavated caverns. People on the train back from Wieliczka thought, embarrassingly for us, that the Bednarczyk children, Zosia 8 and Andrzej 6, were our children. Another cultural specialty was the Polish satirical 'cabaret', at that time one of the very few valves for venting political humour. Needless to say, it was only allowed in a very small cellar!

Finally, an invitation was arranged by my kind Professor Nadachowski for me to spend the Christmas vacation at the holiday house and sanatorium belonging to the Refractories Industry at Żegiestów, a delightful village which nestles in a fold of the High Beskid mountains, part of the Carpathian range, near the elegant 1930s holiday resort of Krynica Zdrój. I was overjoyed to be able to take Anikó too. Our footsteps crunched into a heavy fall of fresh white snow, dampening every sound from the tooting of the train to the rushing torrent of the river far below. We arrived by steam train crawling slowly up the exquisitely beautiful Poprad valley to Żegiestów which overlooks the Polish/Slovak border and a week later we left by train too—the overnight express for the long journey to Warsaw to see the New Year in at the Warsaw Baptist church.

In 1967, Warsaw was still being reconstructed after the Second World War, a full 22 years after fighting finished! Stalin's special gift to the Polish people, for which they paid heavily, was the wedding cake building known as the Palace of Culture and Science. From the top, you get the finest view in Warsaw (it is only from there that you can not see this monstrosity). However, much of the former Jewish ghetto still existed in a very battered state with the toothy look of a Warsaw 'Harlem' about it. It was worse in the clear light of morning because the terror of the blitzed buildings, shattered but still inhabited, was highlighted by the ironic purity of a sprinkling of freshly-fallen snow.

Later that New Year's Eve, we joined a great party of young folk to pray together for God's blessing on Warsaw, on us, and on Poland as 1967 turned to 1968. Little did we dream then how God would answer our prayers. I have often thought how many times God uses those who dare to pray to answer their own prayers!

At any rate, God was giving me the right girl to be my wife. I was Episcopal Anglican; she was Free Church Baptist. I was from an island nation culture; she from a mid-European landlocked one. My experience of working with students had been gained in England and in Poland; she speaking English, as well as Hungarian and German, Slovak and Polish, had been the one to look after the African and other foreign students who came to Budapest to study and who found their way to her church. Her father had warned her about marrying a foreign student—- but he graciously relented when I appeared!

Anikó and I had actually met for the first time in the home of Krzysztof and Ludmiła Bednarczyk in Cracow in the dark winter days of 1967. I was invited to speak at the large Sunday morning student meeting at the Dominican Church, in their cellar known as the 'Beczka' (Barrel), but I 'happened' to meet Krzysztof out shopping in the town during the week. He later took me to a most inspiring Bible study meeting he attended also in the Catholic Intelligence Club at the same Dominican Church, and through which I also met the present Pope (when he was known as Karol Wojtyła, the Cardinal Archbishop of Cracow). But on this occasion Krzysztof told me that he was expecting a Hungarian on Sunday, and would I care to join them for lunch? Never having met a Hungarian in my life, I jumped at the offer, little imagining the life-long consequences!

Anikó wore a heavy long green winter coat and peered at me from behind her spectacles. I was slightly amused by her archaic English—she had been reading an Authorised or King James version of the Bible and did not realise that many of the expressions and turns of phrase in it were no longer in current use and that using them made her sound like a character out of Shakespeare! At any rate, she was naïve enough to invite me to visit Hungary, never thinking that I would take up the invitation.

Five months later, however, when summer came and I had never seen any other East or Mid-European country apart from Poland, I found her address, and wrote to announce my arrival! She arranged accommodation for me with a couple of elderly sisters in her church for the weekend but made the fatal mistake of asking me to buy some medicine for an old lady in the congregation when I was in Switzerland for Dr. Hans Bürki's IFES summer camp. The camp was formative for me, in that I met students and leaders from all around the world and had time to reflect on much excellent teaching. Afterwards, I bought the necessary medication, and by then I was committed to taking it back to Hungary en route to Poland for my second academic year!

The old lady eventually died, probably more from poverty and poor housing than from any illness, but I was easily persuaded to stay in Budapest for a week. Anikó took time off from work at the Hungarian Patent Agency where she was employed, showed me round the city...as my wife she later took British nationality in addition to Hungarian, while I, born in London, am now able to travel on my Hungarian passport.

Bare Foot Doctor at Work

I do not possess the job description or any list of the qualifications needed by Bare Foot Doctors. These are the people famous for being the paramedics widely employed in China to treat the population up-country, well beyond the reach of a health centre or hospital. Obviously, the Bare Foot Doc has to deal with all manner of common ailments—and family problems too. Chua Wee Hian, who followed Stacey Woods as General Secretary of the IFES, rightly described many of his field staff as 'Bare Foot Doctors'!

If we had been wiser, we might not have rushed in 'where angels fear to tread'. Not knowing the correct way of doing things, we just made contact with all the friends we had across Eastern Europe, with their friends and with all their suggestions of likely people—Christian students who could be interested in growing in Christ and in reaching fellow students. We visited pastors of all sorts of churches in every town in every country which came within our orbit. They did sometimes ask probing questions. They must have often wondered just whose agents we were. But they were unfailingly courteous and often received us with overwhelmingly generous hospitality. The pastors knew the key students in their congregations, the enthusiastic ones, whom we wanted to train and equip to be even more enthusiastic and involved in being Christian witnesses to their peers.

Travelling to find the right people also gave us a unique perspective on the realities of the local church situation. I remember being absolutely astonished to enter a large Baptist church in Bucharest and see young soldiers—in uniform—sitting there! Surely they should not be in church? Well, maybe not according to the Romanian communist state, but God was evidently over Ceaucescu, and was giving the churches in Romania a time of revival. The churches were filling with soldiers and all sorts of other young people, and no one, but no one, could stop the Holy Spirit from doing his work. It was a great lesson which I was to treasure. God *will* build his Church, and the gates of hell shall not prevail against it.

Certainly the summer visit in 1993 was particularly challenging and called on all my expertise as a Bare Foot Doctor. Our work camp at Bielice was just that—hard work. We set out to transform the farmhouse at Bielice. We've been working on it for all of 20 years, so we know what it is to decorate—even to re-decorate! We developed expertise at digging foundations, became capable at mixing concrete and by 1994 finally discovered we could even cope with tiling.

A large group of young people from the English School at Voorschoten in Holland had been to view the work in the summer of 1991. They enjoyed the sightseeing, but were less than impressed with the facilities. These are now vastly improved with more showers, a renovated kitchen and cellars, a large meeting room and a coffee bar finished in varnished wood complete with coffee and cream, cakes and chocolates.

The overall picture is enhanced by a brand new footbridge over the river and a new roof on the house. The courtyard has been levelled and walled with huge stones. Our Ukrainian friend, Pavlo Glavnik, who learnt his building skills in the Soviet Army, carried out the work.

In 1992 we worked hard, inspired by Bible studies in the life of Moses. Dr Donaldson, (from New Zealand, but attached to St Helen's Church, Bishopsgate, in London) also repaired broken picks, shovels, forks and other work tools. A certain amount of sightseeing also encouraged the workers.

The following year your Bare Foot Doc turned up well-prepared with more Old Testament Bible studies in my little black bag, only to find that the 'patient' was needing a different kind of tonic. The building work was almost complete, but we were more limited by lack of building materials because of lack of funds! Moreover, there were almost 80 of us—a bigger team than could comfortably work on a project of this size—and many of those who had come (or more correctly, whom God had sent) had probably never heard the Gospel explained before. So we turned our attention to organising an evangelistic camp!

Fortunately I had with me the notes of the one short evangelistic talk I had worked through for the Voorschoten folk's Sunday service, and then I had 24 hours before another was needed, and so on through the 10 day camp. Trained experts may need less than a working day to get their lecture together but Bare Foot Doctors who have not been to theological seminary, need to think pretty hard and long to gather material for even a short Gospel explanation. Add to that the fact that the audience came from six nations and included Ernst Pfeifle, a consular attaché from Germany and no fewer than ten members of St Helen's Church (used to sitting under the excellent expository preaching of Prebendary Dick Lucas and the likes of the Reverend David Jackman, of the London based Proclamation Trust), and you will realise that I was shaking in my shoes and praying hard for guidance and a clear head.

What did all these critics think? I always hope that Christians are praying for the poor fellow who gets up to speak for Christ, or give testimony as to how Jesus Christ has made a difference in his life. It really helps—if they pray they may be less critical! People from my home church in England, and in particular our pastor's son, Paul Markby, have been faithfully and wonderfully supporting me in this way over the past dozen years. On this occasion I did not notice any negative criticism, and it actually seemed as though we were supporting one another. All who wished to do so could take part and share their testimony with the assembled company during our ten days together.

The real glory, however, was to see the joy of the light of the Gospel dawning in the eyes of people who had been far off but were now coming to see the power of the Lord Jesus in their lives, gradually realising that God himself could come into their lives in a personal way through his Holy Spirit, and give them peace and joy and meaning. People in Poland need meaning today. Most of the former landmarks have disappeared. Joy and peace are likewise rare life commodities.

The economic pendulum has swung this way and that. Life was getting better and better under the communist system—at least that was what everyone was told—but it never looked so, and anyone who used their powers of thinking must have wondered if the propaganda experts suffered from schizophrenia. Then came capitalism as the supposed panacea to the nation's problems. At first, everyone was euphoric but quite soon thinking folk noticed the small print, which said prices would rise rather than fall and that inflation would devour any savings in any bank. Unemployment has likewise become a new curse not previously thought of!

Meaning? A few folk have jumped on the 'get rich quick' bandwagon, but serious investment in the economy is considerably lacking. Most young people are now thoroughly confused as to life's meaning. The general economic situation is undoubtedly improving and some of the western glitter of consumer society can be seen in the cities—even if the humble hamburger is still far beyond the pocket of the average Pole as an everyday commodity. Beata Lubicka, a young university administrator writing from Wrocław in September 1994, says: "I finally got the job I like. There is always a problem with money but this is normal. Anyone who wants to live as a good Christian shouldn't get into private business, at least not now." Beata may rightly be afraid of the rush for money squeezing out her spiritual life.

Most Poles are afraid of and prejudiced against the Germans and their intentions. Economic investment and management skills of every description are desperately needed in Poland today but Poles fear the Germans will buy up their industry on the cheap and rule again as they did under Hitler. Poland itself lacks sufficient know-how and finance to pull itself out of 40 years of economic ruin. It is quite common to graduate from university and be unable to find any suitable job at all. The old boy network and corruption, which flourished so well under socialism, are both alive and well.

Some who had a guaranteed job in the old state concerns find no place to work in privatised industry and fall into depression. The jobless rate in Poland stands at around 15 per cent. Private hostels fill with the homeless and the suicide rate rises. Librarians, nurses, teachers and many other public service workers do not like the look of the new capitalism and long for the security their old communist masters gave them. But Jesus can transform lives, open the spiritual dimension, and give a new perspective and wisdom for living. And if he can do that for Poles and build lives which count for him in Polish society today, so he can too for the students who visit us from Poland's neighbouring country, Belarus.

Żenya, one such student, was 16 and an excellent goalie in our camp football competition. In fact 'The Rest of the World' only won their football match against the 'Poland' team because of Żenya's skill and determination, aided by the diversionary tactics provided by a young male calf which wanted to join in the fun. Żenya is a rough-hewn type, as goalies from that part of the world are noted to be. He had only come with his sister from Belarus because their mother had been converted to Christ a short while before and very much wanted her children to attend a camp where they too would hear the Gospel.

Żenya did not seem to come to all the meetings. Was it because there was too much explanation for him to take in at one time? But he listened and responded after I chatted to him in the kitchen, while we were washing up 80 people's greasy plates and the huge pots in which our food had been cooked. His eyes were truly smiling, as they had not smiled a week or ten days earlier. His head nodded in agreement and encouraged me as I spoke. The effects of hearing the Gospel are just amazing. And he was hearing the Gospel in Polish—to him a foreign language—rather like a Spaniard listening to Portuguese or Italian.

I believe, because I have seen it happen many times, that God can cross lots of barriers to bring people into a saving knowledge of Jesus Christ. Who knows, some day Żenya might well be a Bishop or lay leader in his church in Belarus, thanks to an evangelistic holiday camp he came to at Bielice, a tiny hamlet nestling by a rushing stream of clear water in a narrow wooded valley in southern Poland's Golden Mountains. There may not be much gold left in those hills, but there is still the real gold of the Gospel to be told again and to come alive in the hearts and lives of many young people.

Each year since 1985, teams of English students have contributed considerable help and support to the camps as well as to the building. They have bent their backs digging foundations from the rock of those so-called Golden Mountains—and they have faithfully ministered to the campers. In 1993 ten people from St Helen's Church came to Bielice, flying to Berlin and travelling on in two hired cars. Each team member spoke of the way they had come to faith or how God had been at work in their lives, and they all taught English to small groups of the Polish students, using John's Gospel. The camps at Bielice have provided English students with wonderful opportunities for ministry. The warm and friendly holiday atmosphere results in many students, English and Polish, continuing to write or visit each other long after the camps they first attend. Most Polish students are pretty keen to learn English. It is a key to communication and understanding, whether you read law, engineering, computing, music or medicine, or are preparing for the Christian ministry.

CAMPS AND CONFERENCES—PEOPLE AND PLACES

The International Fellowship of Evangelical Students relies heavily on its training camps and conferences for students. Its staff and student group leaders get their training on the job. "By students for students" would be a good motto for the IFES. Camps and conferences are powerful tools in the Bare Foot Doctor's armoury. Over a single week, students can spend longer uninterrupted time considering the Gospel and being taught from the Bible than they would usually spend over a whole academic year.

I have mentioned how in 1969 I had been invited by Stacey Woods to become the student worker for the whole of communist Eastern Europe. In practice, this meant that for the next ten years I travelled to visit and encourage students throughout Bulgaria, Romania, Yugoslavia, Hungary, Czechoslovakia and Poland, with the odd visit to East Germany and the Soviet Union thrown in for good measure. If that was not thin on the ground, tell me what is!

Dr Bürki had made a couple of visits to Eastern Europe in the mid 1960s. Stacey Woods had been in Hungary in the mid 1960s to contact pre-1939 leaders of the student movement. But mine was to be a new pioneering effort after the difficult closed years of Stalin's rule. How was it that God gave Stacey Woods the vision to initiate the student work just then? Certainly Stacey was a man of vision—God had used him wonderfully to kindle the new movement, first in Canada and then in the United States—but Eastern Europe? Surely that was where the Christian Church was under persecution, where Christians were suffering for their faith, where only the ultra brave and/or foolish smuggled Bibles? Some of those who were caught paid the price with long terms in jail. Yet God gave Stacey the vision to begin student work in just such a place.

Christian students were known to exist. Links existed from before the Second World War with previous student leaders in Hungary, for example, which had even boasted a member movement of the fledgling IFES before this body was even properly constituted in 1947. It was many years before Mikhail Gorbachev ruling in the Kremlin brought in the era of openness and restructuring of the old communist system. Aiming for a Marxist social democracy, his glasnost and perestroika, referring to the political and economic reforms in the Soviet Union and its satellites, became the watchwords of the late 1980s. But even back in the 1960s Stacey was thinking that God wanted IFES to begin encouraging Christian students under the communist regime—and he shared his vision with us.

It is said that politics is the art of being in the station when the train comes in. Often you don't even know which station to wait in, but in God's goodness, and through ten years of patient toil, often through danger to ourselves and to others with whom we were involved, this is the story of how God did guide us in working out his plan, so that for the Soviet Union, East Germany, Poland, Czechoslovakia, Hungary, Romania, Bulgaria, and Yugoslavia, there we were ready and in the station when the train of glasnost, perestroika, democratisation and new freedoms arrived. Surely, without living to realise it, Stacey Woods had truly sensed the 'hour of God' for IFES to begin work in Eastern Europe.

Otto von Bismarck is credited with the observation that "Great politicians owe their reputation, if not to pure chance, then to circumstances at least which they themselves could not foresee". Today we see freedom of speech, freedom of religion and assembly, as well as governments chosen by and accountable to the people throughout Eastern Europe. Mikhail Gorbachev was the political figure who brought these freshly discovered ideals for reform to his people's attention. He never anticipated that the clash between the hopes of the peoples and the tired face of the communist structure he represented would cause growing political tension throughout the Soviet bloc, hasten his own loss of influence and ultimately result in his resignation.

Eastern Europe was buzzing with these new ideals in 1987 and pressing to discover their limits and freedoms. In 1989, Gorbachev was lurching to the left, ordering a 500 day reform plan, and then to the right, rejecting the plan and surrounding himself with old party faithfuls. But by then it was too late to go back. Many Christians thank God for using him, like many Old Testament kings, despite himself. What eventually happened illustrates just how God is in sovereign control. By August 19, 1991, Gorbachev was under house arrest and hard-line old communists were trying to seize control. This was the moment of truth for the democratic reforms which Gorbachev had set in motion in the Soviet Union and throughout its satellites. People in every country in Eastern Europe were as concerned for the outcome as were people in Moscow. The thought of again submitting to a government that had seized power through another communist coup caused a chill throughout the Soviet bloc and also in the West. Would we be back to chaos and bloodshed and then another Cold War? But, in God's goodness, that was not to be. Boris Yeltsin emerged as leader of the opposition. Here was the elected president of the Russian Republic standing on top of the tanks in Moscow calling for a general strike. Thousands of protestors joined him. The army paratroopers switched sides and moved to protect the president. After three tense days, God answered many prayers and the coup was over.

Yet back in the 1960s, the communist world in Europe was

only opening ever so slightly. How could I, one person, achieve anything worthwhile in such a vast field with a population of millions, and thousands upon thousands of students scattered in its cities and towns? Students lived in the ancient university cities and in the tiny agricultural colleges in the remote countryside. They were scattered over eight nations speaking as many different languages, while I spoke only one fluently and could stammer a little something in a few more.

If I had been more of a realist, perhaps less starry-eyed, I would probably not have accepted the challenge. As it was, we started from where I had contacts—in Poland—and from where Anikó had contacts—in Hungary—and, under God, the work grew. We visited individual students and encouraged them to link up with other Christian students in their universities and colleges in order to strengthen one another and to reach out with the Gospel to their friends. Stacey inspired us, and we in turn sought to inspire the students. Everyone wants to belong to a winning team, so we drove ourselves hard and "God gave the increase". Being foreigners, we could visit several different churches in the same town without showing any partiality. So despite a general ghetto mentality among the smaller churches in Eastern Europe, we were soon adept at encouraging all the Christian students we could find to join forces.

A Visit to Students in the Soviet Union

One of the most surprising meetings I recall took place in Odessa in May 1972, the main port of the Soviet navy on the Black Sea. Travelling by train from Sofia, the capital of Bulgaria, I was refused a transit visa for Romania. This resulted in an uncomfortable night sitting in a police room on the railway station in Bucharest and my being sent back to Sofia. Two days later I reached Odessa by overnight boat from Varna on Bulgaria's Black Sea coast. Without a single kopek in my pocket, let alone a rouble, and having passed customs, I had to make my way on foot. With my heavy rucksack on my back, I climbed to my obligatory pre-booked hotel up an impressive flight of some 200 steps to the town on the cliff top. If I'd had even a few kopeks I could have taken the lift.

Western tourists were not supposed to wander freely in the Soviet Union. Those watchers or keepers of foreign visitors at Intourist, the Soviet Tourist Agency, were visibly shocked when I walked in to their office as I had not turned up on the train as previously arranged. They did not allow for such unscheduled changes of plan. However, my reserved hotel room was still waiting for me, and they directed me to it. I went to the student dormitory the next day taking the Christian books and the Bibles I had got past the customs. Rucksacks are not all that easy for customs men to explore without being completely emptied. The books were my surprise for the students but, our Bible study over, their surprise for me was a huge pot of stew which had been hidden all the while under the table around which the eight of us had been sitting. Precious fellowship. I am in touch to this day with the leader of that group, who studied not only mathematics but with considerable accomplishment, piano as well.

I would sometimes be invited to speak, at a Sunday service or to a mid-week Bible study group with some students present. We were also on the lookout for Christian students who could benefit from a training course at Mittersill. Some of the brave ones would eventually get permission to travel.

Life in Romania

It was not always expedient to go to a camp so far away as Austria. Amazingly, we were told to try to hold camps in Romania, by a friend of IFES who spoke to me under the cover of a loudly playing radio in his flat in the Romanian capital, Bucharest. He was there from the United States to do historical research. He was convinced his flat was bugged and very probably it was. He described in frantic detail the secret police chasing him and his friends round the boulevards of Bucharest. The Romanian police did not like being made fun of by foreigners!

"The worst that could happen," he told me, "is that, if we have a camp and it is discovered, the foreigners will be thrown out of the country."

"Yes, but what will happen to the students?" I asked him. "Local people will have to stay behind to face the music."

I knew that some Romanians simply did not get in to university if they or their parents were known to be Christians. They failed their exams—quite mysteriously—and even if they were good students, they knew they would never get those helpful extra points for having parents who were factory or farm workers. The children of white collar workers had a more difficult time reaching the grade needed to commence university studies, so some parents would leave their office job and work on the factory floor for a strategic year or so to help their children enter university. On the other hand a bad word from the local party secretary would ruin your chances. So too would attendance at a Christian camp, if discovered by the dreaded officials!

Up in the mountains of Romania in Transylvania, away from it all, surely there would be peace from such spying eyes? Actually, this was unlikely. Some dared to set up printing plants in the city centres where the noise of trams and heavy traffic drowned out that of the illicit presses. Paper deliveries were not noticed where people were coming and going by the hundred along the pavements every hour. Secret workers could be lost in the crowd. Out in the countryside any event such as a student camp would be sure to be easily noticed and it only needed one pair of less than friendly eyes to lead to betrayal and the midnight knock from the dreaded secret police.

A very small amount of publishing was allowed inside Romania. The two bishops of the Hungarian Reformed Church, Gyula Nagy of Cluj and László Papp of Oradea, recorded in "Reformed Church in the Socialist Republic of Romania" in 1976 the production of one book each year from 1945 to 1950, but then very little more than a yearly church diary/calendar in 122,000 copies after that date. The shortage of Bibles intensified but, they boast, "It is befitting to mention that throughout this period (since 1945) we have not published the Bible since in this respect we enjoyed the brotherly help of the World Reformed Alliance—which sent us 10,000 Bibles in 1971."

There is not a word of complaint in this account in fact quite the opposite. "Let us express our respect and gratitude to the wise Government of our Socialist Country for the manifold support granted to us" (the description glows or fawns!) "over the past 30 years, in the great transformations of the life, being led by the will to achieve social justice and human solidarity. The achievements which we describe were made possible because our State has secured for us the necessary freedom to carry out our Christian duties." Then, just in case you missed the point, they continue, "Our Church has enjoyed this freedom..." No great surprise, then, that these two ignoble fawning tools of Ceaucescu' s State disappeared abroad immediately after the Revolution of 1989.

The home of Romanian student friends to whom I had taken some precious Christian books was raided and the books were confiscated by the police—despite being well concealed. Other students had found it simply impossible to even begin any higher education due to their known Christian stand at school. The long strong arm of the Romanian secret service was not to be taken lightly. The worst that might happen to me would be to be expelled. I would then be unable to visit, to befriend and encourage any more students and my ministry could be finished!

Arne and Ingeborg Kappelgaard from Copenhagen bravely lived in Bucharest from 1982 to 1984—yet the terror of the Securitate watchers they endured then still gives them fearful shudders almost 20 years later.

Arne told me how, after they married in 1977, they went to two conferences at Mittersill. *"When we were invited to Mittersill the following year as team members on the student conference, we were planning to use the next two weeks to visit friends in Hungary, Poland and Czechoslovakia. But before we'd made any arrangements Brede Kristensen asked us to go to Romania for exactly the same period. Ingeborg was studying education, and was also the Mission Secretary in the KFS, Kristeligt Forbund for Studerende (the*

Danish IFES movement), while I was studying theology. Because you, Alex, had been refused entry to Romania, it seemed very practical, having travelled so far south from Denmark to Mittersill, for us to go on to Romania.

"I recall how you were taken by surprise in Mittersill, and dug deep in your memory for addresses. You found a good few and also suggested a couple of tourist sights worth visiting. Brede helpfully reminded us that Christ is the only legitimate Lord, even in Romania. So when we work for him we have no reason to fear or have a bad conscience. That gave us tremendous strength to withstand the pressure which could sometimes come from suspicious authorities.

"Our first visit to Romania made a great impression on us. In the first home we entered, in Cluj, Pastor Dan straight away closed the curtains. We arrived in the evening, as you'd told us to. We said 'Pace' (peace) and then stood in a circle to pray. After that we could say who we were!

"The next day we were invited to give a greeting in the Cluj Baptist church from which Pastor Dan had recently retired. It was moving to sing 'My peace I give unto you' to a church where the congregation spilled over into the courtyard and outside the building.

"We also visited the Pentecostal church in Cluj, and that was where we heard singing in tongues for the first time. It was like a cry from Revelation, lifting us up from the pains of this world into heaven.

"One of the young people we spoke to turned out to be in the group of politically active Christians. They were claiming human rights and equality in those difficult years. This man had the idea of making a film of the student work in Romania to send to IFES. The Securitate, however, saw us with him and when we continued on our journey a Securitate man dressed rather like a mountain climber joined us on the train and openly interrogated us for three hours.

"At first we did not want to talk with the 'climber', but soon sensed that it would be better to appear to be open with him. So we told him that we had not wanted to speak with him because he was

speaking in German, and we both come from a part of Denmark which had been occupied by the Germans. Now we could make use of one of those two tourist spots about which you had told us to explain of why we wanted to go to the little town of Deva—nearby is the ruin of Hunedoara castle, which everyone would agree is well worth a visit.

"'But where will you go after that?' he continued. Ingeborg replied, 'Arne is interested in history, but I would like to go sunbathing, so we can not agree where we are going.' He could not draw us further. Fortunately we were advised by a local person to take a bus for the last 20km to Deva instead of going in another train, so the Christian family who had set out to meet us at the railway station were saved from being compromised by our visit as they could not meet us!

"Later, when we went to Timişoara, we still felt that we were under close scrutiny. There we ran into another politically active Christian, Ioan. We also had our first contacts with African students in Timişoara. Two years later not one of those politically active Christians were still in Romania. They had all been put under such pressure that they had no choice but to emigrate. I did later meet one who had been politically active in Iaşi, but he had been trained by Navigators coming in from the West. The Navigator had told him, 'You must choose between political activity and spiritual growth. You can not have both'. 'And now, years later', he said, 'I thank them that they forced me to choose.'

"At that time, 1978, Iosef Ţon had returned to Romania with a PhD from Oxford. He was pastor in Oradea, but also preached regularly in Cluj. Iosef was a mighty inspiration to all people, especially students. He taught on a wide variety of topics they had not considered before. Ioan, the politically active man in Timişoara who helped to draw up the Charter '78 for human rights, said about Iosef, 'He's not joining our group but has expressed his sympathy with us. He tries to be the first among preachers, the first among politicians and the first among radicals. He should only be a radical.'

"Iosef Ţon managed to stay for a few more years before he was forced to leave Romania. I heard a sermon by him on 'Why are

we having difficulties?' He said that sometimes it is because God needs us to do something and we suffer for his sake. Sometimes other people need us to do something which can be painful for us and sometimes we suffer because we need it. 'I tell you, I have no enemies,' said Iosef, 'absolutely no enemies,' yet everybody knew that the Securitate were giving Iosef all sorts of problems. Rumours were planted in his church that he was secretly co-operating with the authorities. This was their tactic to make nobody trust anyone else. Iosef said, 'Remember the stone quarry. There is so much noise there, mining, hammering, sawing the stone. Every stone is cut to exactly the right shape and then put in place to make a fine building, the temple of our God. So I tell you again, I have no enemies, I have only workers in God's quarry.' That sermon made a great impression on me.

"The main link Ingeborg and I had was with the African students. There were 10,000 of them in Romania at that time, from many different countries. Originally they were invited to Eastern Europe so as to sow socialist ideas in Africa. Later some East European countries saw educating them as a way of making money out of their governments. Neither the Romanians nor the Africans were ever very happy with the arrangements. Most Romanians were very racist in their attitudes, yet they also envied Africans and Middle Easterners because they could use the black market to live well in Romania.

"Most ordinary Romanians did not realise the extent of the difficulties the Africans faced. Two laws made it almost impossible for Africans to have contact with Romanian students. First, it was not allowed for Romanians to have foreigners stay overnight without prior police permission. Breaking this law could cost a Romanian a fine of two months wages. Second, Romanians had to report after they ever spoke to foreigners. They had to tell the police each time what they'd talked about. While this law was not always enforced it certainly discouraged Romanians from inviting foreign students into their homes. An African medical student from Timişoara who we invited to Denmark told us that only then, for the first time in seven years, did he visit a family in their home.

"That first visit, in the summer of 1978 was really a test by

fire for Ingeborg and me, so you can imagine how we felt when you, Alex, visited us a few months later in Copenhagen and suggested that we might study for a year in Eastern Europe. We had been planning to go to Africa, and when our colleague Ada Lum suggested that we go to Greece we said, 'No way!' But when you talked about Eastern Europe you suggested that I might go to study theology through official channels. You said, 'Hungary would be much easier, but since you love Romania perhaps you should go there.' And we thought, 'What? Have we a love for Romania?' We had not felt it but through that remark our love was kindled. It felt like you were blowing into a little fire and the flame shot up.

"So it was that we returned to Bucharest for twelve months to study at the Orthodox Institute of Theology and I visited Romania almost every year from 1978 to 1991 and we never had such frightening experiences as we endured on our first trip.

Africans in Bucharest

Arne's story continued:—*"In our flat in Bucharest, in a building housing only foreign students, no Romanians were allowed to visit us, but we could make a home for Christian African students to come and relax with us.*

"We held a weekly Bible study group for our friends, and this became a real inspiration for all of us. Once, one of the Africans said that he'd been followed all the way to our home, and the Romanian 'watcher' entered our home together with the African. The Romanian told us that he had to check our bathroom, because water was running into the flat below. This was so obviously an excuse to see just who was in our flat and probably to let us know they knew something was going on. Several times this African was told at his university department that they knew about his contacts with us. One day one of his teachers said in the middle of a lecture, 'then there are those who go where they drink stimulating drinks and play the guitar.' Shortly before this the warden in our house had visited us 15 minutes before our usual Bible study time and we had offered him a cup of tea, obviously the stimulating drink!

"Some of the Africans were very active missionaries, visiting

Romanian congregations, going with young Romanians on evangelistic trips to other churches and broadening the horizons of Romanians by giving them glimpses of God's worldwide Church. We were very happy to encourage them.

"Newton Njeru from Kenya was one of the most enthusiastic missionaries. He had twinkling eyes, which made him look like a fox. Newton described how he returned from Mittersill to Romania with a hundred books in his luggage in 1980. The customs officer said, 'You will not be allowed to take more than one copy of each' and he started going through the 100 books. He found 98 different titles, plus one English and one Romanian Bible. The customs officer kept the books but Newton complained to the customs when he was back in Braşov telling them that the books were his personal possessions. Eventually they had to admit that they could only keep the Romanian Bible.

"Newton said, with a smile, that new African students at the forestry school were told, "You should not be like Newton." He was constantly witnessing. The police called him in several times and suggested that he should stay with his own church instead of visiting so many. Newton explained that he was an Anglican, but there was no such Church in Romania. Then the police said, "You are allowed to be a Christian, but can't you keep quiet?" Newton replied, "Don't you know what Christianity is? It is part of Christianity that you have to tell the good news to others." And he started telling the police.

"But," said Newton, "When you talk with policemen in a dark street they like to listen, one at a time, privately. In the classroom I cannot say anything. One teacher tried to hurt me by saying unkind things about Christians but I'd decided to say nothing, and just to sit and smile at her. This provoked her, yet I continued to smile. Eventually she said, 'Look at him, just sitting and smiling.' She became so furious she had to leave the classroom."

"Newton's fellow students asked him how he could stand it. Later he had a great opportunity to explain what it meant to be a Christian. We felt that the Christian students were Daniels in a lions den—we were just there to encourage and support them by opening our home.

"Newton was once invited to a Christian wedding in a village. The whole village were invited but few of them were Christians. The family asked Newton to give a good speech. As an outsider he did not need to be careful, so he gave a powerful evangelistic talk on the parable of the wedding party.

"Once we expected Newton to join us for an evangelistic tour to the Black Sea but I did not find him when I went that evening to meet him off the train from Braşov. Early the next morning Dorte, then aged 2, woke up and went into the sitting room. She returned to us in our bedroom saying that a black man was asleep on the sofa. I said, "No, you must be mistaken. I did not find him last night." "But he is there," she said. And, sure enough, there was Newton, fast asleep on the sofa. His train had been delayed. It arrived in Bucharest at 1 a.m.. By 3 a.m. he reached our home. We could not hear the bell from our bedroom but for once we had forgotten to lock our front door. Newton said, "God knew I needed a place to sleep."

"Towards the end of our stay, during the summer holidays in 1982, we decided to hold a weekend 'camp' in our flat. We invited 35 students from all over Romania by word of mouth. Newton said to me, "You know it is dangerous, don't you?" I replied, "We'd nearly forgotten that." We had been having Bible studies every week but only for African students. I said, "We'd better pray that God will protect us, or should we cancel the camp." "No!" said Newton, "I just wanted you to start praying." So we prayed that only ten people would come. Then we decided to make it a birthday party for three days, because we were a family of three and we would need lots of birthday speeches. In the end exactly ten students turned up.

"Once, when I visited Newton in Braşov he took me up the mountain in the ski lift at Poiana Braşov. We ascended to the restaurant, 100 metres below the peak. Then I suggested we climb those hundred metres to the top. He'd never been there—Africans only walk when they have to. As we reached the peak he suddenly saw a fantastic view over the Carpathian mountains and exclaimed, "Wow, I must bring my group up and have a prayer meeting with them on top of this mountain!"

"It was much harder for African girls to live a Christian life in

Romania. Being cut off from family and social life and having no one to care for them made them feel like lonely trees. It was very un-African and very hard. Fortunately there were few African girls anyway but we had to advise some of them to return home.

Arne continued, *"I visited Cristie Ţepeş in Iaşi a few times. Cristie was the leader of a student group which was unusually outgoing. They would often go out to a village after Sunday morning worship to witness. Cristie would take his guitar on the train and they would sing Christian songs along the way. If the train conductor came and asked them to stop, Cristie would politely stop at once but continue after they had changed trains.*

"On other Sundays they would go to a home for the handicapped, and take them out in their wheelchairs. Once I went with this group to the botanical garden in Iaşi to have a Bible study. As we began, a drunken guard came and troubled us. Cristie spoke with him for an hour.

"I used all Ada Lum's techniques to help Cristie create a Bible study. Afterwards he said, "How interesting it has again become to study the Bible." He felt as though he'd been running dry though actually he was an unusually good student leader.

"Right after the Revolution, in 1989, Cristie was invited with other Christians to work in the Department of Cults. He refused to take a salary, but took the responsibility in this transition period. He had wanted to leave his work as an engineer and go abroad for a two year course in theology but instead accepted this call to make Christian programmes for Romanian TV. Cristie told me later that in their team of 14 TV producers for those Christian programmes all the other people were nominally Orthodox but interested in almost anything except Christianity.

Ingeborg Kappelgaard then shared with me, *"When we arrived in Romania we decided not to use the black market so as to understand and identify with the Christians who were very consistent in not using it.*

"We arrived at our two room flat only to discover that there was

almost no furniture because Arne had refused to pay a bribe. So we used my rucksack and some boxes as chairs! After a couple of months we received the furniture that we were entitled to.

"We did not depend so much on material things but it was very cold that September. However, the rule was that the central heating would only come on in October. When we went shopping I never knew what I'd be able to buy—toilet paper, tomatoes or carrots. A friend was coming from Denmark and we prayed earnestly that I'd be able to find some eggs to bake a cake. I was as happy as if I'd won a million when I found a tray of eggs! I made a big cake but our friend was shocked. "Why have you used up all the eggs?" she asked. "We're going to have a party, and tomorrow can take care of itself," I replied. We learned to trust God for all the little things of life and our friend remembers that too.

"We felt that our two small rooms were luxurious. I spent a lot of time in queues for food with Dorte, aged two, alongside me in her pram. Someone once asked where I came from. "From Denmark," I replied. "Do you have to wait in queues there for food?" "No." "Are you satisfied, do you like living here?" I said that I'd found friends in Romania and there were many things I did like. I avoided saying anything bad. But then a man said, "Why do you ask that? Who is paying for your stay? Is it the Romanian Government? Why are you here?" And I could say, "We were invited by the Orthodox Church but the Lutheran World Federation is paying for us." No more questions! We had to learn to distinguish between the spies, the Securitate and the ordinary people who were just curious.

"Once I cried because I'd spent half an hour in the wrong queue in a shop. I was sent back to another queue to pay. I was so miserable but someone said, "Come on," and she helped me. This experience helped me to learn how to help others with psychological problems—women I need to help now, years later. God used these experiences to prepare me for the work he would give me with immigrants in Denmark in 1999.

"I prayed a lot that we would find a family with a child Dorte's age, around two, so that she could have a natural friendship. In the building where we lived I met Marcel, Louis and Ramez, aged 2 from Egypt. They were Coptic evangelicals and seemed to have

suffered from being in a minority. Ramez and Dorte became good friends, speaking Arabic, English, Romanian and Danish all mixed up. After a while Ramez said to his parents that he would like to visit Dorte's church. So they came along with us to the Anglican Church.

"I became good friends with Marcel, and once asked, "Are you evangelising among Muslims in Egypt?" She replied, "They have their faith, and we have ours. A Muslim cannot become a Christian, it would be very dangerous." So I told her about a book which was fascinating me, "I Dared to Call Him Father". She read it, and when it came time for her to return to Egypt she asked, "May I take this book with me?" I said, "Is it not too dangerous?" Marcel said, "I believe now that God can protect me. I would like to share it with some Muslim friends."

"When we said 'goodbye' to them I was so moved that I cried. Louis said it was the first time he'd seen a European cry on such an occasion. Those tears dissolved some bitterness. They came as foreign students and felt out of place, but they helped us a lot and made our lives in Bucharest easier.

Beginning of Books and End of an Era for Arne

Arne continued his story, *"Rodica Cocar was a student from Sibiu whose father was a Baptist pastor. Courageously she trained as an opera singer. The system in Socialist Romania was for graduates to be assigned a job. "Fortunately," she said, "the opera could not use me. I was free to choose my own job."*

"Rodica chose to become a secretary at the Baptist centre in Bucharest. There she translated the evangelistic Bible study series "Jesus, One of Us" which had been written by students co-ordinated by Ada Lum. It took ten years for it to be published. We tried to publish it outside Romania after checking inside the country but

this delayed the process considerably. We felt discouraged as it could have been of great use to student Bible study groups.

"After the 1989 Revolution it was possible to publish Christian literature inside Romania, but it took time to establish a publishing house. The concept of these Bible studies was so completely foreign to normal Romanian thinking because there were no definitive answers, right or wrong. It was said that in Romania you had to be a born again Christian before you could think independently. The teaching tradition was authoritative and by rote throughout society including the Church. But student groups who saw the book were enthusiastic. IFES had been working with Operation Mobilisation to make solid Christian literature available in Eastern Europe by encouraging writing by local authors. However, in Romania it was impossible to publish locally written material so authors had little incentive to write.

"Fred Bailey, who worked with the Austrian IFES affiliated student movement ÖSM in Vienna, and I visited student leaders in Timişoara in April 1990. We found perhaps the strongest Christian student group in Europe with 40 Bible study group leaders. They told us how in the early days of the demonstrations in December, 1989, Christian students were present alongside many other Christian people. When they had no more voice to shout they stayed at home to pray. They told us, "We've had visits from around fifty Western Christian organisations, at least five of them aimed at students, so now let us hear what you have to offer." Fred told them very clearly, "We can offer no money, we have no fixed programme and no international headquarters telling us what to do. But if you want to build a national Christian student movement we could share some experiences of others in the same situation and we could offer some training and materials to help so that you can make your student work independent." "That is new. No one else told us that," they said.

"We also found a student group in Cluj which had started to publish its own magazine so expertly that people did not believe it was produced in Romania. They did excellent art work in their eight pages. One of their secrets was that a student's father worked at a paper mill and the paper was of unusually high quality.

"A national Romanian student movement emerged and was accepted into IFES in 1998. Four or five cities each had their own idea of what a Christian student movement should be and it took time to unite them into a national movement. In Iaşi, for example, they were open to having Orthodox people in the student work; others were frightened by this.

"The final meeting of the IFES team of people who visited Eastern Europe took place in Mittersill in 1991. Now there were people present from all over the area itself and Fred Bailey made it clear that this marked the end of us visiting to help the work.

Arne concluded *"One night there at Mittersill I had a dream. In the dream I was lying in bed. I felt my feet getting cold, and the cold crept up my body. I knew I was dying. I lay there, fully conscious, and said 'goodbye' to all my friends around me. I knew my visits to Romania had come to an end. It had always been a spiritual feast to meet Romanian Christians, and it had been humbling, and yet it had always been a tremendous strain for me to go there. So at the same time I felt relief as well as a loss, a death, a sorrow at the close of the time when I was part of IFES.*

Broken Leg and Unblocked Toilet in Poland

In the early days camps could beheld in some countries. It happened with great secrecy and care concerning who was invited in Bulgaria and Czechoslovakia and with somewhat less anxiety in Hungary and Poland. Even so, there was often an element of danger. The Król brothers, Adam and Henio, and their sister, Nina, all later university teachers and fine Christian leaders, decided to organise an evangelistic camp for their student friends in Poland. It was not easy to make sure they would not be interrupted. They did not have a large enough property available so they decided to book an entire hostel.

Nina told me:

"We lived in Silesia in difficult times. My mother's family always lived in the same house in Katowice. Her brother was born two years before her and the house was in Germany. She was born two years later in the same room and it was in Poland. So she had a Polish birth certificate, although they spoke German at home and she went to a German school.

"My father went to a Polish school in Cieszyn, which had been Austrian but then it became Polish and there were strong Czech connections. Then the war came and Cieszyn was German, but they spoke Polish.

"Later he studied in Lwów, which was Polish, then when the second World War started he could have been taken into Germany, but there was a firm in Gliwice where a Christian boss employed Poles and Jews to stop them being deported to Germany. My father found himself in Gliwice and the daughter of that boss became my mother, though she was only 16 at the time.

"The big house that my grandfather built in Gliwice when it had been in Germany became our family home even though my parents lost everything through the war. Afterwards a lawyer, who was not a Christian, said my parents should have the house back and eventually with his help my parents bought back their house from the State although it was completely ruined. My father was asked to work for a construction firm in Gliwice with payment in the form of goods to repair the house. When she saw cart after cart drawn by horses arriving with sand and cement, wood and glass, to repair our house, my mother cried for joy.

"There had been a spiritual revival in the Cieszyn area before the war, that affected my parents though we came from a background where there were very few Christians. In our town, Gliwice, we did not know of any other Christian family. Our parents had told us that we were not on this earth just to enjoy ourselves—we were here because God was our purpose in life and we had to tell others about the only true life that exists in God. The only problem was that it seemed prohibited at that time to even mention the word 'God'—so how do you do it?

"Eventually as students we became friends with people asking about the purpose of life; that was a very good beginning. We

needed to bring them to the Word of God and we needed time to do it. We started meeting for birthday parties. We were not allowed to have Bible meetings so whenever anybody had a birthday we would invite all our friends to tea on Sunday. My father was teaching where we studied, at the Silesian Polytechnic in Gliwice, and used to invite students as well. We ended up by having up to 50 students in our home.

"My father would say that we should share the best that we have, so we did, and the very best was the Word of God. There were some very dangerous moments but the Lord blessed our work. It grew quietly and soon we were having weekly meetings where the Bible was always read. Some people seemed to be waking up to the Bible. Then my brothers and I were invited to England for a Christian house party. That was the first time we were in a free atmosphere. We could even go out on to the street and sing a Christian song or be on the beach and sing. We were also encouraged by the consistency of English Christians and came back eager to share this with our friends.

"It was then that we had the idea of a ski camp. This would be the reason we could give the authorities. We told each of our friends that it would be a Christian ski camp. They were not sure what they were letting themselves in for but as they all liked skiing that would do. Such a camp would have to be registered, so it was a holiday ski camp and we made sure we had a registered ski instructor with us. I was near the end of my studies in architecture, my brother Adam was in the middle and Henio was in his first year. The guest list filled up quickly. The Lord was sent us a couple of Christians from abroad and they were able to inject a lot of good content. This is important as students are thinking people, trying to understand things, and they appreciate good teaching. There was no literature, no prepared Bible studies, nothing apart from our Bibles. It was 1966, just before the new edition of the Polish Bible was published, so not everyone had a Bible, particularly our Catholic friends.

"Two students came who were very active in Swedish Inter-Varsity. This was such a great encouragement to us. We didn't ask them their surnames, they were just Stefan and Stefan. Even when

you, Alex, came on to the scene the following year, we just knew you as a friend and a student of ceramics in Cracow but gradually it came through that you also had the Christian motivation and we learnt more about IFES.

"We held that camp in a hostel in Kozince near Gubalonka in the Wisła area, a very pretty part of the country. The lady who ran the tourist hostel was very suspicious when we wanted to hire the whole place for a whole week. Adam and Henio, told her that our students would be serious young people who saw more in life than just having fun. She was very sceptical but gradually warmed to us and agreed to rent us the hostel. But two days before the camp we heard that a girl from Katowice had enroled who was the daughter of one of the secret police chiefs and who was related to the lady warden. It seemed an absolute blow. Although we planned to do nothing wrong the spiritual battle was on. It could have cost all of us our positions as students in the Polytechnic. I remember us praying together in our parents' bedroom. "O, Lord, this is it. It seems that we are all finished. But you, Lord, know what to do, and we leave it with you." Then the miracle happened. We hadn't prayed for it, but the girl fell on the ice, broke her leg and was in hospital. When we saw her she had it in plaster. From then on we started to pray that she would be saved anyway, even though she wouldn't be able to take part in the camp.

"Everybody arrived not knowing each other and not knowing what to expect. Our Swedish visitors blended in extremely well. They were so motivated by the love of God and reverence to God. We had a very full programme including skiing and the warden warmed to us day by day. In the end she said she'd never come across such a group of people, and what was it that made us so different? In such places away from home people often misbehave very badly. This is what the lady had been afraid of. On the first day everyone realised there was a problem with the toilets. She said there always was. The following day she was absolutely astonished, because in the evening the boys had taken some acid, cleaned and unblocked the toilets properly and cleaned the whole washroom. It was clean from then on till the end of the camp. That was what convinced the lady; she could see there was something different

about our people. They were consistent, not only talking about things. She heard about the Lord but chose not to tell others because she was a party member. But she came to many of our meetings and from then on the door was always open for us to go to that tourist hostel. It was such a very joyful camp with lots of singing and it was great when we returned to Gliwice because everyone was now much more keen on Bible studies.

"Singing seemed such a good way to reach lots of people so we formed a music group, DEOdecyma, with which we toured from 1975. This led in 1986 to establishing a music recording studio which became DEOrecordings. We now act as agents for several Christian music publishers in Poland and the Commonwealth of Independent States, the former Soviet Union. In 1996 radio was a natural progression. Radio CCM (Contemporary Christian Music), has one of its transmitters at Kozince where we had our first student camp."

The Vision for Bielice

Narrow escapes, such as the episode with the daughter of the secret police chief, prompted other students to look for a place they could call their own where they could hope to be left more in peace with their friends. So the vision for the house at Bielice was born, the end of the conversion of which is just in sight as I write these lines some 20 years later. It lies in a narrow valley just at the gate to the 'Golden Mountains' National Park—a truly superb location.

When I first drove up the valley the hoar frost was heavy on the pine trees, the snow was deep and crunchy, icicles hung from all the village houses and the old mill stream, which in summer gushes joyfully over the rocks was now gurgling and struggling along under a layer of ice. In a curious way I always look forward to the challenge of Bielice in the snow. Will it be so deep that we won't be able to drive up to the house? I have used chains often on the last 12 km of the journey, up from Stronie Śląskie, and that is just the beginning of the adventure!

The house is always snug and warm and the valley sparkles in the sunlight under intense winter blue skies. Then there is that satisfying silence that the noise-dampening snow always gives. The waterfalls, especially up in the National Park, freeze into static, shining sculptures and you hope no little children are playing near when the amazing icicles, up to a metre long, start to fall off on a sunny day. Little flocks of tiny brownish red/black Bramblings and lighter coloured Chaffinches sing and fly together with their characteristic bounding, dancing flight among the hornbeam trees around the house or off over the little fields beyond the stream towards the wood which leads up to the Czech border where the deer or a silver fox come down in the middle of winter. The place oozes quiet and seclusion from the rush and stress of city life where students spend most of their time studying and preparing for examinations. The ever-changing colours of the woods and fields and the endlessly different effects of clouds and sky never fail to lift my spirit to heaven with thankfulness. No wonder that students also find it often easier to come close to God in a place demonstrating such outstanding beauty of his creation.

Drawing of house at Bielice—

where cowslips bloom in profusion in all the meadows and on every bank as soon as the warmth of spring chases winter's snows away. Where wild fungi abound on the forest floor and wild raspberries are ready in September, but a profusion of blueberries welcome August visitors—do they taste better in Poland, or just over the border? Bielice is only 1 km from Czech territory.

Wardens for Bielice

God called Gustaw Muszkiet and his young wife, Maria, to care for the farm, the house and the visitors to Bielice for the first 7 years of its life as a student holiday conference centre. Gustaw told me how this came about. It was no romantic call for him.

"I worked as a foundryman" he said, "in a metallurgical factory in Skoczów making castings for motor car engines. Maria taught Russian at a school in Wisła. After we married in the summer of 1976 we went for our honeymoon to Giżycko in the wonderfully beautiful Polish lake district. There we met Ela Zachanowicz. Ela told us about the house at Bielice, which her brother Witold and their Uncle Stefan had recently found and were negotiating to purchase. They were looking for someone to be the warden, work the farm and care for the house and the visitors. It wasn't a proposition to us at that point, just the question 'did we know someone'. We both already had jobs and a flat and we led the youth group at the Lutheran Church in Skoczów but the idea of Bielice which Ela presented appealed to us and we said that we'd pray about it.

"Later that year Witold Zachanowicz travelled for nine hours from Wrocław to Skoczów to see us. They had not found anyone to be the warden but would we please come to see the village and the house at Bielice and perhaps agree to stay as the 'owners', as the purchase had already been agreed. We went later that autumn. It was cold and grey and the rain was pouring down. Through the swirling mists we could just about make out the house where they were proposing that we should live. The weather was terrible and the empty house looked like a complete ruin. There was nothing we could like about it. Yet, though so cold and uninviting, we felt that if it was God's will we should be prepared to go.

"So it was that, in March 1977, we took over as the owners of the ancient farmhouse 'Bielice 5'. Maria taught till June, then, the school year over, we went to Bielice. It was a difficult time but we learnt so much. We saw God at work and received many blessings.

As a young, newly married couple, far from any helpful fellowship, it was a time when we needed to seek God's will and learn to rely just on him. Our first son, Dawid, was born after we'd been there just a few months. We were in the middle of the re-building work. Brothers from the church in Wrocław came to do the work but for us it was a time to seek the will of God in many little ways. We bought our first cow and started out into farming. We experienced the truth of Genesis 3,19 - "By the sweat of your brow you will eat your food." Our experiences with farm work were fresh and new and from time to time God sent us people who could be blessed, even by working alongside us.

"Ordinary people came into God's kingdom - that was our greatest joy. Sometimes it was at a group holiday, a camp. These were led by many different people, from Wrocław, from Gdańsk, the Król brothers from Gliwice or Krzysztof Bednarczyk from Cracow. Other individuals came, sent by God we believe, when there was no youth camp on. We led an ordinary Christian life and after they had been living with us and helping us for a while, visitors would sometimes ask, "what do we need to do to be saved?"

"Niusia Zachanowicz and her brother Witold often came bringing their friends, classmates and teachers. I recall one particular group, brought by a young friend of the Król brothers. Romek Janaszak came from a Christian family, and was about to finish his secondary schooling. He realised that none of his class had really heard about Jesus. He told me that as in May he would take his exams and finish at the secondary technical mining school in Mikołów could he please invite his whole class to Bielice. So around 40 young people came late in May, 1980. They were all aged 18 and very hungry for spiritual life. The boys helped me on the farm, looking after the sheep and chopping wood, while the girls helped in the house, cleaning and cooking. In the evenings we read the Bible, sang round the camp fire - and several received Christ as their own saviour. When they returned there was a group who met together for prayer and they joined the Lutheran church in Mikolów.

"More than once a whole class came. Niusia brought her whole class from their Grammar School in Wrocław together with their headmaster. On another occasion she took them for a similar holiday

in the Lutheran minister's house at Karpacz, but often she would come to Bielice with some of her classmates. Some of her friends were converted. Her physics teacher noticed the difference in these girls and asked why it was. They gave their testimony very naturally and told him they were going to Bielice for their winter holidays. That teacher, now the headmaster, also came with his wife and their little children. The Król brothers were at that camp, and we had lots of question and answer sessions.

"During our seven years at Bielice three children were born Dawid, Estera and Anna (later they were joined by Daniel and Jakub). That time prepared us for further service for God at Oleśin, outside Warsaw, but we always look back with thanks to God for all we experienced there. In particular Stefan Zachanowicz was a great blessing. He had worked as an inspector of buildings, so he knew how to arrange the supply of all the materials we needed - almost everything was hard to get hold of in those days. Matthew 6:33 became very precious during those years of shortages and of blessings. We had it written on the wall in our flat after we married, "Seek first his kingdom and his righteousness and all these things will be given to you as well."

The Story of Witold Zachanowicz

I have been to many so called 'camps'. Some were held by the students in relatives' homes, another in a woodcutter's house above Wisła, and in holiday villas in Jagniątków in the Karkonosze mountains near Jelenia Góra, even in a fire station (used by Dick Dowsett, the speaker who I took along with me from OMF, more to light spiritual fires than to put physical fires out!) and in the old farmhouse at Bielice. But one memorable summer camp was exactly that, a canvas camp organised by Witold Zachanowicz and his brother-in-law Żiutek Modzelewski in a field by a farmhouse near the Baltic coast north of Gdańsk at the delightfully named village of Karwieńskie Błoto—Karwia's Swamp! We cooked over a wood burning stove in an outhouse. Keeping the heat up was quite a feat and we had meetings sitting on bales of straw in a barn. Yet this somewhat primitive camp was seminal in the growth of the work. Students came, were inspired to take leadership in the work and the good effects of that camp ripple outwards to another generation.

Many students have moved on to other work. Student work has never been considered an end in itself, but rather a way to share with students how they can reach out to others in the lecture room and the laboratory; and those who they meet on the games field and in the student dormitory. The short term aim is to build and strengthen the faith of Christian students and others who are still on their spiritual journey to Jesus Christ. The ultimate aim must be to strengthen the churches students will go to when they graduate. Interdenominational Christian student work might also promote good inter-church relations! Witold was a Baptist, Żiutek was a Pentecostal.

Witold was the one to whom God gave the particular vision for the student camp and conference centre at Bielice. He writes how the vision came about:

"I feel really privileged to have witnessed some of God's history being unfolded before my eyes, years ago and even today. I have always believed that God is in control, even when it seems that He may not be. I was born and raised in a small town called Hajnówka in eastern Poland, a very peculiar kind of town where the population was part Polish and part Russian part Ukrainian and part Belorussian. The little Baptist church which my parents attended was similar. Some of the hymns were sung in one Slavic language, some in another. The same was true of all the sermons (up to ten on any one Sunday!) by whichever of the men were moved to do so. As you can see, I was brought up in a wonderful mixture of Slavic traditions which were devoid of typically Polish nationalism. Had I been born just 200 km more to the west in Warsaw I'm sure my outlook would have been totally different.

"My Russian maternal grandfather was one of the founders of the church in Białowieża. He was a very interesting man. He trusted in Jesus, but had a drinking problem. In his youth he had been a soldier in the Red Army and took part in the 'Great October

Revolution' (which brought the communists to power in Russia). Later on he was captured by some of General Pilsudski's Polish troops and finally settled down in Białowieża and Hajnówka.

"When I was 12 or 13 years old, God put a deep interest in his Word into my heart. The Kircuns, who were pastoring our little church at that time, stimulated that interest by leading us through very interesting Sunday School lessons and youth meetings. As a 14-year-old boy I was just dying to meet with other young Christians, to talk and discuss things with them. You can only imagine my joy when my parents decided to move to the city of Wrocław where we children could attend schools and where there was a much bigger, active Baptist congregation. To our surprise, Alek and Halina Kircun decided to transfer to the same city too.

"The next phase of my life was filled with all sorts of high school activities and making new friends at school and at church, but somehow the activities of our small youth group were the most important to me. At that time God called me to put my trust in him and to commit myself to serve him. I have fond memories of all the other young people who discovered the faith and shared their youthful enthusiasm with me. We were close and would spend communist May Day holidays together, usually on trips to the mountains where we would sing Christian songs and have short Bible studies. The 1st of May was when everybody was supposed to be marching in a worker's parade! We would also hold fellowship meetings on New Year's Eve when the whole country seemed to be drowning in vodka.

"At that time that many of us saw a need to have a place of our own that would be dedicated to studying God's Word; somewhere our non-Christian friends could be invited and where we could share our faith in a non-church environment. It was difficult in Catholic Poland to invite a friend to some 'obscure' evangelical fellowship. That is how summer and winter Christian camps in Poland were started in our school holidays. We were not ashamed of our little churches but somehow it was much easier to communicate in the relaxed atmosphere of a winter ski camp in the mountains or in summer when we were together somewhere on the Baltic coast.

"There were several leaders who would organise such camps.

Sometimes they would invite popular Christian speakers from other countries, at other times they would provide the teaching themselves. The first camps organised by the Król family were really popular with the students and blessed by God. Other people who were active at this time were Henryk Wieja, Janek Lisztwan, and the Wojnar brothers, Jan and Nelek. Some leaders of the Baptist, United Evangelical, and Lutheran churches were quite supportive, especially Józef Prower and Krzysztof Bednarczyk. Some of these leaders had good Christian friends who were most helpful in providing us with speakers, Bible study materials or food supplies.

"You, Alex, were one of those from 'the other half of the world'. I had a really good chuckle when you mentioned that some people suspected you of being a spy. It sounds so ridiculous now, but in those dark days the mistrust that the enemy of God managed to plant in people's hearts was so deep that...even I, who knew you and your family so well, worried that you might be used by someone for such a purpose, because you probably were very good 'spy material'.

"I remember the expression which Ron Davies (now Dr Ronald Davies, recently retired as Director of the Postgraduate Centre for Mission Studies at All Nations Christian College, England) used with reference to your 'agent-like' activities and the fact that you used to appear and disappear rather suddenly: "Alex is like Gandalf". Gandalf is a character in J.R.R.Tolkien's stories who does exactly the same: appears and disappears suddenly as he tries to help others. On the other hand, I do not blame people such as Alek Kircun for having had such ugly thoughts, for they too had suffered a lot of emotional stress at the hands of the 'angels' of the Urząd Bezpieczeństwa, the State Security Police.

"At the end of the 1960s and into the 1970s, more and more of us had the opportunity to visit western countries. My first trip to the West was in 1970 at the invitation of a Swedish Christian organisation with ties to the World Council of Churches. I went to their winter conference expecting that most of the time would be spent on Bible based discussion, singing and having good fun on the ski slopes but it turned out to be an endless deliberation on how to solve the world's social problems and the possible implica-

tions of the Russian invasion of Czechoslovakia on the world peace movement. Somehow I could not grasp those ideas and was a little disappointed with the whole conference.

"After finishing my high school I went on to study civil engineering at the Wrocław Polytechnic. That was a busy time as far as church and youth activities were concerned. When it became possible for me to study at All Nations Christian College I was so happy, even though that meant interrupting my regular studies. As I look back on that year spent in England I am grateful to all the people who made it possible. You and Anikó were patient with me when I so frequently visited your home in Newick. I enjoyed sharing in your family life, watching David and Andrew grow and seeing the way you juggled family life, Christian work and hospitality which you extended to such people as myself.

"Later in the 1970's more and more Christian students from Poland were able to attend all sorts of courses in England or Austria. My most memorable experiences were of providing interpretation from English into Polish for our large group of Polish students. The speed of the lectures and the torrent of new, never before translated ideas just made my head spin. The Polish participants enjoyed the more Bible based lectures best. Some of the teaching relating to social and cultural issues was less relevant.

"I had to decide whether to continue with my civil engineering studies, or go in a different direction. After a lot of soul-searching I decided to study English and become a teacher. At about the same time God gave us another wonderful opportunity. An old farm was bought in the tiny village of Bielice with the idea of converting it to permanent facilities for Christian camps and conferences. The initial money was given to us by some Christian churches in America, thanks to the efforts of John Alexander of the Inter-Varsity Christian Fellowship of the USA. Little did we know what an enormous undertaking we were letting ourselves in for. The beginnings of this project were small. Every little step had to be overcome with great difficulty.

"Originally the farm house was to be for the benefit of any group of Christian students. However it was only when the local Baptist church in Wrocław gave us more support that the whole

project gained some momentum and became what it is now: a place for young people, children and other Christians which has, under Polish circumstances, pretty good lodging, cooking and recreational facilities, complete with a ski slope and the most picturesque surroundings. Praise the Lord for the efforts of such people as Uncle Stefan (Zachanowicz) who has literally put his life into it."

Both those initiators, Witold Zachanowicz and Żiutek Modzelewski, have moved on to other good work for the Lord but God called Adam Cenian, then a physics undergraduate, into student work at that camp with Ada Lum and Ron Davies in Karwia's Swamp. While a student Adam was active among fellow foreign students. Later, he became chairman of his church—which allowed him to lead a brigade of willing hands to build a new church largely with their own hands. Still in academic life as a post-doctoral research physicist with the Polish Academy of Science (he sells Bibles from his room at the Academy), Adam and his wife Nelly, who teaches piano, have also continued to have much contact with students and have regularly, with a fine team, led inspired evangelistic and work camps at Bielice.

Some Realities of Life in Eastern Europe

Poorly paid East Europeans tend to judge a person less on salary and more on individual achievement. If you are a scientist or a teacher you doubtless appreciate such an attitude. Top scientists are world class. Recently many have acquired a peculiar habit: every year they spend a few months working in a Western laboratory. Adam Cenian, for example, has an excellent link with a professor in the physics department at the Free University in Berlin. Every spring he can be found along Unter den Eichen (Under the Oaks) a street by the Berlin Botanical Garden. He is not there to admire the greenery, but to keep in touch with world physics and to earn extra income. Theoreticians need little more than their computers but others also need equipment. There is simply not enough money to pay for both salaries and equipment and a month or so abroad is a good stop-gap, a far better solution than losing these skilled people altogether. Far too many have already been lost to science and become repair men or computer salesmen at much higher salaries than the prestigious Academy of Sciences can afford.

Even today there are still signs of counter-selection which dragged Eastern Europe down during four decades of government controlled economy. Positions of leadership tended to be filled not by the best qualified but by those who could be relied on to carry out directives handed down from above. The area of scientific research was probably the one most resistant to this syndrome but even here its effects still linger. From my friend Mirosław Grylicki at the Institute for Refractory Materials in Gliwice I heard of the communist manager of a refractories plant who took refractory bricks to build his new house. All was well until those bricks, designed as furnace linings, disintegrated to a sticky mud when attacked by the rain!

Another continuing weakness is the poor work habits of many. Before the return to free market economies, salaries were largely independent of job performance. Many employees habitually tended to their private affairs during regular working hours; some would even take on a simultaneous second job. Today more are working hard, but some have been slow to change. Personnel may gather round a desk during working hours to enjoy a leisurely meal, coffee and conversation—and work related interruptions are definitely not appreciated. I learnt of a laboratory facing deadlines where one worker decided to re-build his car. Poles joke that 'Fiat' stands for 'Fix It All the Time'. Two Polish plants produce Fiat cars under licence from Italy. For several weeks he only put in token appearances at the laboratory. Then he decided he needed a holiday week but it turned out that he was away for three more weeks. But he still considers himself a decent hard-working person.

Professor Andrzej Kielski told me of a young man who stole his car and, being rather drunk, soon crashed it into a tree. The young man was devastated when he found out that he knew Tomek, Andrzej's son. "I'd never have stolen it if I'd realised it was yours," was his rejoinder. But, being a mechanic, he arranged for it to be repaired and it was returned to Andrzej Kielski's garage. Then Professor Kielski noticed that it needed its annual roadworthiness test. "I'll fix that for you too, sir," said the thief. And he did. The test certificate arrived in the post—but to his great surprise the car never left the garage under Professor Kielski's Cracow home.

Poles know that this East European 'system' will reap them rewards—in hell. One story concerns a man who held dual nationality, British and Polish. When he died he went to hell. It turned out that there was a choice—capitalist hell, or communist hell.

"I've lived all my life under this terrible communist regime," he says, "I'll try the capitalist hell." Capitalist hell turns out to be a smart skyscraper. He enters and enquires where he needs to go.

"Take the lift to the fifth floor, go to room 540, and they will tell you your punishment there," is the answer. He takes the lift, finds the room and inside it a clerk is seated at a computer. He gives his name and after a keying in a few strokes she says,

"You will be boiled in oil for a thousand years, every night you must sleep on a bed of nails and every day the nails will be sharpened."

"Oh, just a moment," says our friend, thinking to himself that it might be just as well to investigate what is on offer in the other place. He makes a quick exit via the lift, and walks across to the communist hell.

In communist hell the building is crumbling and hasn't seen a coat of fresh grey paint in 45 years. The fittings are archaic, notices are stuck on the walls with sticky tape and the whole place is laden with gloom—but after all, it is hell. The lady at reception is cleaning her nails and doing her hair. He waits in the queue while she phones her boyfriend. Eventually she tells him he can not come in without getting his documents in order. He has to see the doctor to get the stamp in his identity card showing that he is now deceased. He has to get another stamp to show he finished at his factory. It takes time, because these offices are not open each day, so he spends a night in a hotel and comes back the following morning. Now the receptionist tells him to go to the fourth floor. The lift is broken, so he climbs the ill-lit staircase. He peers along the fourth floor corridor, she hadn't told him which room to try. He tries a door, and finds another lost soul who tells him he should really go to room 540 on the fifth floor. He trudges up and is surprised that this office is open. A gush of cigarette smoke greets him as he opens the door. An unruly crowd presses round the counter. The secretary has files everywhere, she opens a cupboard and has to push the files back as they threaten to fall out. He waits and at long last gives his name and ask for his punishment.

"Oh, yes," says the secretary, "I've been expecting you." She searches through piles of files on her table, along the counter and finally finds it—underneath the telephone!

"You will be boiled in oil for a thousand years, every night you must sleep on a bed of nails and every day the nails will be sharpened."

"That is just as bad as in the capitalist hell!" he cries.

"Oh no, not at all." She replies. "We have no money to pay for coal to heat the oil. In any case the stoker has been off sick for ages and the functionary who sharpens the nails went off to a production conference and no-one knows when he will be back."

Back at the time we camped in Karwia's Swamp, meat was rationed and hard to get. How kind we thought the farmer was when he agreed provide us with a whole calf all nicely cut up into suitable portions. We would never have noticed but one student's father was a butcher—almost a quarter of the animal had not been delivered. We pointed this out to the farmer. Did he blush? Only ever so slightly. Poles do sometimes cheat each other, not only foreigners. Foreigners do need to be specially alert in public places and on public transport. It is well known that Warsaw taxi drivers pick up fares at the international airport with meters already showing a large sum from a previous journey. At your destination, you may just think that Warsaw taxis are frightfully expensive!

Waiters likewise doctor their bills if they think they will get away with it. I heard recently of the date being added to the bill and misusing an electric cash register to do so! The threat of reporting this Gdańsk hotel restaurant to the police brought the immediate offer of a completely free meal for the whole party of six.

Likewise keep both your eyes on your luggage at all times! Turn round on the railway platform and your suitcase may well vanish. Fall asleep in a long distance coach and your belongings may disappear from the rack. You may also regret the long time spent reporting your loss to the police!

I well recall one such occasion. Győző Kmethy, my future brother-in-law, arrived by train in Cracow from Budapest. Anikó and I met him and we went to visit Krzysztof and Ludmiła Bednarczyk who lived in a flat high up in ulica Zacsisze (Quiet Street), a few minutes walk from the railway station. With Győző's enormously heavy case to carry, our arms were straining even before we reached the long flights of stairs up to the Bednarczyk's flat. We dragged the case to the second floor. It was dark. We had not seen anyone. Nor did we. We left the case, ascended two more floors and chatted briefly to our friends at their front door. But by the time we returned the case had vanished.

"It must be inside one of those three doors on the second floor," I told the nonchalant policeman at the station half an hour later but he was not prepared to leave his cosy office to come and see. He supplied forms for us to fill in but the process dragged on and we felt we were just wasting time. After a couple of fruitless hours translating between Hungarian and English and then getting the right words down on the form in Polish we were exasperated. Would we hear from him if they found the suitcase? "Oh yes, we'll let you know if we find it," the policeman replied, "and you let us know if you find it!"

Camps Begin in Croatia

One of the most dedicated families to run camps for students was the Jonkes of Zagreb in Croatia. Their generosity extended to purchasing a house and fitting it out to accommodate 30 to 40 students in the simplest style. We helped on the 'spiritual' side with evangelistic talks and in many practical ways as well. The house lay below a dam at the end of the tiny village of Lokve on the edge of a national park around 100 km south of Zagreb and 20 km from Rijeka. Tall, pale christmas roses had escaped from the national park and were blooming across the fields and meadows in late spring. By September cyclamen were flowering under the trees and the meadows were boasting a host of autumn crocuses. The lake formed by the dam provided wonderful boating and swimming. The national park and surrounding countryside were as good as Bielice for walks and excursions and almost everything was to hand, either in Lokve itself or in Rijeka.

Meat was no problem if you could face entering the local butcher's shop, into which the beasts themselves also walked to be slaughtered. I was never there personally when this was going on, but a very vivid painting of an ox tied up in this very shop and about to become beefsteak hung on one wall! We have forgotten the more precise meaning of the word 'butcher' in our day when meat can be chilled, carried from place to place in refrigerated vans, and produced in identical slices all hygienically film wrapped for sale in the supermarket.

Lokve took you back 50 years. The first time there we learnt how to cook on a barbecue. It was not a luxury but a sheer necessity. We needed to install a wood burning cooking stove with a special long chimney to also radiate extra heat to the big room next to the kitchen. This was purchased in Zagreb but the Jonkes did not have a suitable car to transport it. Our Mini van was small but designed to take goods, and the hefty wood burning stove just fitted into the back. Off we set with three of us, Anikó, me, and Nada Jonke across the two front seats. We were amused when she remarked we were going quite slowly! As we drove along the short stretch of motorway out of Zagreb towards Karlovac the speedometer was reading 50 or 60. "My husband and our boys all drive so fast," she complained. "You are wonderful to go so slowly," she continued not realising that our English vehicle was showing miles per hour! She would have had a fright if she'd realised we were approaching 100 km per hour.

Let Nada tell the story of how they came to Lokve:

"I would like to tell you about the barracks we used for 17 or 18 years here in Lokve. I don't recall just which year it was but I had seven or eight children, four of ours and some from the assembly, at a youth camp at Zeltweg in Austria. Afterwards the young people asked "Nada, why do we have to go outside? Why can't we have it here in our country?" The same idea was already in my own heart, so we asked around in our assembly if anyone knew a place for such a camp. Mary my sister said to go to a family near Lokve where they used to go for holidays and talk to Nada Pinta, who had a lovely meadow—and there it was. The first year we were there with seven tents. We made it but it was wet and very difficult. Dado Berković and his father and mother were with us, that was 1967 or 68. We cooked in Nada's kitchen and slept in the tents but it was uncomfortable.

"The next year we returned to Nada's meadow but with just one tent. But it was raining so hard we couldn't even put the tent up. One of the children said "Ask Teta Nada if we could put our beds under the roof of the little wooden barrack she has." "Yes," she said and her son made us a ladder. It was so dirty: underneath was a stable and upstairs the hay-loft. The boys used the ladder and slept there and I slept in Nada's house with the girls.

"Then something very significant happened. My husband, Gabriel, said he would go for a walk with the children. I do not like to walk much but this time I said I'd come too but they went off without me. I was amazed but I went to the lake above Lokve alone for a walk. It must have been the purpose of the Lord because as I came up to the dam the sun was just going down and there was a wonderful picture on the lake—I could just see the garment

of the Lord enfolding me over the lake and for a while I was lost in worship. Then I turned and could see this simple little wooden house, the barrack where we were staying and this ladder. I had to pray. "Lord, you who were born in a stable, buy this cottage for your people! It is old and ruined but buy it for your people, Amen." At that moment my husband arrived with the children so I told him what had happened. Immediately he led us down to Teta Nada, and announced in her kitchen "We will buy this cottage." "Is that so?," she said, "is that so? We just wanted to pull it down, because it is good for nothing." But there, for the whole of these 17 or 18 years, there has been life, life, life. Nothing organised but just life. I cannot tell you how so many people came from so many countries. Once a bus arrived with 25 Americans! Deary me, where could I put them? We already had as many people staying. I cannot explain it, but lunch was enough for everyone. They all ate, they were happy and they went off. It was really an abundance of love. We started in 1969 and slowly it built up. We always came in summer. I was longing for something in better condition, something built from brick. When we told this to Nada Pinta she said: "Well, we really need this little cottage, because our grandchildren have nowhere to come over the summer." I replied, "Teta Nada, you are right, of course you can have it!" because I was already desiring to get a better place. "OK, after a year," she agreed. But the next year, she said, "You can be here this year too," and so we stayed. And then Gabriel brought a big bouquet of flowers and I said: "You see the fine way we will go out from this palace." And the five or six year old grandson of Teta Nada came, and I asked him, "Did you see this royal bouquet?" "Oh no," he replied. "Come along, I'll show you". "Oh, how nice," he said, and then asked, "and where is your king?" "Well," I said, "of course he's in heaven." He went out of the tiny cottage and said to his grandmother, "Their king is God!" That's the last thing we heard in this cottage—not: "You can just go." It made such an impact: "Their king is God."

"Our friend Roger Forster came from England once with his little boy, who said: "This is a real chicken house." But the Lord has put many chickens under his wings. We had meetings after almost every meal and many young people said: "If there had

not been Lokve, I don't know where I would be. I got the spiritual foundation for my life here." And many good marriages began in Lokve. Through this little cottage, there is now a nice house as a drug-addict-rehabilitation centre. Like the apostle John: "I write to you children, I write to you young men, because the word of God is in you," and they have to be strong to subdue the devil. "And I write to you fathers." And now we have nice fellowship with the people round here. We have prayers and Bible study with half a dozen people, and do drama with the children. And I distribute cassettes with Bible verses which their own children made. Now there is a period of quietness through Gabriel being ill but people still come for Bible study."

Croatian Fruit

Nada Jonke's son, Tomislav, is a church leader in Zagreb today and also runs the rehabilitation centre in Lokve. He takes up the story about the grounding in the scriptures and the Christian life which he received through IFES camps at Mittersill.

"I remember so well every little detail of that lovely castle in Mittersill, the guest speakers and their themes, such as pollution and the principles of Bible study, the beautiful mountain setting, the fellowship we enjoyed together, the sauna and the 'apfelsaft' (apple juice, as much an Austrian speciality as the sauna!)

"Days spent there were vital to my spiritual growth. At that time a group of twenty young people were having problems in our local church. It was becoming very exclusive and closed, hardly in touch with the real world. Later on we were kicked out!

"The Schloss Mittersill fellowship was a real light in our darkness and difficulties, showing us that there is no need for any sharp or artificial division between the Christian world and the rest of God's creation and that we need not be sad and unhappy in order to demonstrate our sanctification. Together with many other youngsters I discovered real fellowship with our God. In a word Mittersill established my walk with the Lord in the right direction.

"I am very thankful to God, primarily for stabilising my faith in him for those with the vision of bringing us youngsters together and to many people who helped in different ways. The principles of studying the Bible in groups, with a mind open towards God, his Book, and those in the group were very helpful later on in our evangelistic Bible study groups."

Daniel (Dado) Berković was another of those young people who, as a physics student, came to Bible courses at Mittersill and to summer camps at Lokve. Daniel has worked for three years part-time developing the foundation and constitution of the newly launched Croatian Bible Society. Now he teaches Old Testament at the Evangelical Theological Faculty in Osijek. This school was started by Peter Kuzmić in 1974 in Zagreb as the Biblical Theological Institute but later moved to Osijek, where Peter is still its director. Daniel told me:

"We are training R.E. teachers who attend a two year course. I also teach Old Testament and Hebrew to full time students working on a four year degree course at the University of Osijek, as well as short-term diploma students and the Bible Education by Extension (BEE) programme throughout ex-Yugoslavia, Croatia and Romania.

"Half a dozen young pastors or missionaries recently graduated from this school: God is blessing church life. War produced a strong impetus for people to search for eternal life and meaning. We have so many refugees—lost in space and time—with nothing but their thoughts. People now are far less materialistic because they irrevocably lost so many goods. There is so much work for spiritual pastors, evangelists and leaders not only here in Croatia but also in Bosnia where I have also been teaching.

"Dozens, if not hundreds of new Christians, ex-Muslims and others in Mostar are eager to grow in their new found faith. Mostar Evangelical Church has 150 people, one third each of ex-Muslims, ex-Orthodox and ex-Catholics. Before the war the church was slowly growing with around 50 people. Those 50 fled as refugees if they were not killed. The pastor had to leave and a new work was started

almost from scratch. The new pastor, one of the students from our seminary who I taught for two years in BEE, planted the church. He is an evangelist and missionary and has now moved on to new church planting in Bihać, Tuzla and Sarajevo, while another of our former students has taken over the pastorate in Mostar. In Tuzla, there are already 23 baptised believers and 45 attending. Several new believers say they were converted through their relationships with Christians who provided relief aid earlier in the war. There were no known Christian believers in Tuzla prior to the fighting.

"I was brought up in a Protestant home in the middle of a very Catholic country which now is Croatia. My mother was a member of a free Brethren Church, an evangelical church, so I was basically brought to the church from the cradle and attended church very regularly. I became a real Christian when I was 17 when I understood what it was all about and I honestly can say that I gave my life to Jesus. A year later I was introduced to the Christian conference place in Mittersill by IFES. So the first time I visited Mittersill was in 1973. The friendship link which brought me there was the late Chris Davies, who was on IFES staff for Eastern Europe ex-Yugoslavia and the Balkan countries. I have been there at least once every year. I consider myself to be almost a piece of the furniture at Mittersill!

"The beautiful views of the Austrian alps certainly help but you find there what I would dare to call the 'Spirit of Mittersill'—the fellowship, the vision, the idea behind the place and the people there making it work. There is the family environment, working together, being together in the fellowship of Christians, being friends without any divisions, and working to help Christian students.

"Chris Davies was a special person for the whole of ex-Yugoslavia and Croatia. She was a tremendous friend, not at all patronising, but humbly serving people in this part of the world. She was one of the best people we ever had. She suggested that I study theology at London Bible College.

"The same vision stood behind the camps we had at Lokve. Again the idea was to bring young Christians together, regardless of their confession, to give them the chance to live and work together and to motivate and equip them for future ministry, whatever and

wherever that might be. I must underline that it was all due to the vision of the people who started these places. Both drew people from their own countries and from abroad.

"Mittersill for me was fellowship and working together. In 1979 I worked in the kitchen and on building a path around part of the castle for five months. We worked as a team, growing together through working together. That experience didn't come till I had been attending spiritual events, courses and seminars, for at least five years. At those events students discovered friends from around the world; and I met my wife from England, the sole member of an IFES Graduate Team in Amsterdam. There were some regular lecturers and houseparents (the Catherwood family would be remembered by many participants) and a very humble servant and excellent pianist, Marilyn Knapp, who has given so much as a volunteer almost each year.

"I was greatly helped through meeting and learning to understand young people from many very different cultures. Seeing their interests and needs challenged me to understand their intellectual needs as Christian students. This helped me later when I studied in London as a foreign student myself and later as a teacher of theology and as a pastor. In other words I was helped to understand how to meet the needs of young thinking Christian men and women. I started a pastoral prayer breakfast where between 10 and 30 evangelical pastors and leaders of para-church organisations like Operation Mobilisation, Campus Crusade for Christ and IFES come to share and encourage one another. There is a full-time Croat staff worker for IFES work now in Zagreb."

Chris Davies reactivates student work in Hungary

The left hand did not know what the right hand was doing! Chris Davies was very busy in Hungary but Daniel Berković, just over the border in Croatia, knew nothing about that (neither would it have been wise for him to do so). Before the Second World War there had been a vibrant Christian student movement in Hungary. Now memories hardly survived twenty-five long years of communist rule but Chris Davies had a vision and was working for the dawning of a new day.

Dr. Kornél Herjeczki, in 1996 chairman of the Hungarian Fellowship of Evangelical Students, explains how the new baby was being reared:

"I began my studies at the Medical University in Budapest in 1977, and Zoltán Kovács kept on inviting me to a meeting which he called a student Bible study group. Christian students from various denominations would come together to study the Bible and to pray for each other and for their non-Christian friends. For two whole years I did not attend once, because I just could not understand why such meetings were necessary at all! I was very active in my own church, particularly in the young people's group, and had little time for other meetings.

"Eventually I did decide to go. We were supposedly celebrating a name's day, although there was actually no one present who had that particular name! The political situation was such that it would not have been possible or safe to organise a larger meeting in a private home for Christian students, especially with a guest present from the West. He or she would be considered by the authorities to be a potential enemy. There must have been something like 25 of us altogether. A young lady from England, whom I did not know at that time, by the name of Chris Davies, asked us to read the story of the Last Supper. Then she put some questions and we had a discussion about Jesus, the disciples, and what all this had to do with us. With the help of these questions, we discovered things that had never occurred to me before... After this, I was present at every meeting, eventually becoming the president of MEKDSz (the Hungarian Fellowship of Evangelical Students) which came into being in an official form from these initial efforts. My own experiences greatly helped me to understand the reticence or reluctance shown by others, not to be shocked by it but to trust God that in his good time he would convince them of the importance of this work, just as he had me.

"What was Chris Davies' historic mission? The walls separating

the various denominations in Hungary were much more formidable than they are today. Chris decided to visit the evangelical churches in Hungary in a systematic fashion, looking for and enlisting those students who - on the basis of personal talks - she reckoned were interested in student work. They would then gather at a special monthly meeting and gradually got to know each other. After a few weeks of this activity Chris returned home to London, but she continued her ministry, writing long letters in which she would advise and encourage the students. I am very grateful to God that I was one of these. There were many others. It was Chris who 'discovered' Dóra Bernhardt, who 15 years later, was secretary of MEKDSz. It was Chris who introduced Dóra to student work and so her influence is still being felt today.

"Chris was conscious of having been called by God to do this work. It was not easy under the prevailing political situation. Chris would often say how glad she was that, as a foreigner, she did not have to know everything and so was free to ask questions and make comments. She also found it an advantage that, being a woman, she was not taken that seriously in some Christian circles and this gave her more freedom to seek out students, pastors and people in positions of leadership who were interested in student work.

"Chris was also a strategic thinker about the long term importance and significance of student mission in Hungary. She may well have been the first to suggest the founding of a Christian publishing house in Eastern Europe for the purposes of mission. As it turned out, she lived to see the establishment of both MEKDSz and the Harmat publishing house though as for their development, due to her untimely death at the age of 43 in March, 1992, she can watch only from heaven. We do not understand why it had to be like this but we accept it as God's will. Chris was a wonderful example how God sends the right people at the right time. She was obedient to God, and God could use her tremendously in his work. We shall always treasure her memory as that of a blessed servant of God.

"It was also of tremendous importance that students were able to take part in the international student conferences at Mittersill year after year. At that time it was something rather special to go to

a Western country. This alone made the conferences attractive but we received a great deal more than just a trip to the West.

"Mittersill was where we could gain insights on how to evangelize students and how to organise and run retreats or conferences. All this was completely unknown in Hungary at that time.

"For decades, the common understanding had been that spiritual life is to be lived out just within the four walls of the churches. The socialist state had succeeded in brainwashing people to such an extent that, when starting our student mission, we had no idea that there had ever been such work in Hungary. All that was enveloped in a shroud of silence. I recall meeting the pastor of a church who, it turned out, had been a student leader in Hungary prior to the Second World War. When we started doing student work in the 1980s he told me, "We no longer need anything like a student mission in Hungary, you need not bother..."

"It was Chris who provided us from England, from a British library, the documents relating to an international Inter-Varsity student conference held in Budapest in 1934 predating IFES. We also received from England a list of the Hungarian participants and the correspondence sent from Hungary in connection with that conference!

"Mittersill's huge significance was that, year by year, about half a dozen students would come home bringing with them the conviction that student work had to, and could be, conducted in Hungary. It was enormously helpful that they were not only told about this but that they were also able to take part in such work. During these conferences they could see that problems were much the same all over the world but also that our God is the same. We integrated, as basic principles, what we learnt at Mittersill and that was the blueprint for our activities back home.

"I want to mention just a few things of unique value for us from IFES and Mittersill. Firstly, it is not run by pastors, who are about to retire, but by students. It is completely voluntary, and people are not doing it because someone keeps telling them to. This impressed me greatly. It also guarantees that the work will stay fresh and 'student like'. The talks at Mittersill were always of a very high standard, both from a spiritual and an intellectual point of view. We

learnt that it was all right to ask questions, and that we need not try to 'shelter' the Bible from questions. It was at Mittersill that we learnt how to study the Bible in small groups. This was completely new for us. We had never heard the like, let alone seen examples of it! We developed a taste for it and saw excellent examples of how to lead these small groups.

"We also heard - to our great surprise - that it was also all right to read the Bible with non-Christians! This is what we call an evangelistic Bible study. We could hardly believe our ears when we heard that, contrary to our usual experience of many Christian students going to university and losing their faith it was quite possible to enter university as an atheist and to become a Christian before finishing your studies.

"We experienced at Mittersill the joy of meeting Hungarian Christian students from other denominations who were just as committed to serve God as we were. We found that it was possible to be one in Christ. It required no special effort to simply be together and work together and this helped to eliminate many superfluous and harmful dividing walls.

"Last but not least, we saw wonderful models of spiritual leaders. Chris Davies and others were wonderful examples of how to lead. I used to think that a leader always has to be up front, has to do everything and has to know what to say on every topic. Starting from such a point of view and knowing my own limitations, it would never have occurred to me that I could ever be a leader! However, I came to recognise that being a leader does not mean that you do everything. It is possible to lead in such a way that people don't even realise who the leader is! It was at Mittersill that I not only heard of this, but I also saw it in practice. Had I not done so, I certainly would not be where and what I am today.

"In conclusion let me share a personal experience: I first met my wife in Mittersill. Yes, we both came from Hungary but we had never met and did not show particular interest in each other at the conference or for seven more years. However, we were both involved in MEKDSz and now we have been married for seven years. We are very grateful to God for each other. Mittersill will always have a special place in our hearts."

Let Stacey Woods have the last word. Without knowing it, Kornél Herjeczki was echoing many of his ideas. Stacey writing in 1978 in "The Growth of a Work of God"[20] about the doctrinal basis says:

"The need for taking such a firm position goes back to the last century when the Cambridge Inter-Collegiate Christian Union, took its stand regarding the necessity of adhering to the conviction that the shed blood of Christ, his substitutionary death, was the one and only basis of reconciliation between God and man." He continues[21] "Today as never before we need an unchanging point of reference outside ourselves, one which is objective and eternal. We need "skyhooks" that link us from earth to heaven, from time to eternity. Without such a lodestar, such unchanging points of reference, a movement is adrift and lost, and its ministry ceases to have meaning and direction. Life becomes "an encounter with nothingness." And Stacey concludes[22] "So the basis of faith (of the Inter-Varsity Christian Fellowship) continues to be not some tattered banner to be revered as something significant for the past, not some meaningless relic, but the basic, active, undergirding element of the entire movement, its structure and its ministry.

"At the heart of the movement its raison d'être is the conviction that the Bible is God's Word. What the Bible said God said. The Scriptures are entirely trustworthy in all their parts, not just in matters of doctrine but when properly understood in all references to space, time, persons and events in this world. Being God's Word inspired by the Holy Spirit, it carries the absolute authority of God.

"We thank God that in his grace and goodness he has kept the...movements true to this basis, to God's Word, and to the Lord himself. May the Lord Jesus so sustain us true to him until with joy we humbly greet him in his second advent."

MOVING ON

Towards the end of my ten year stint, working with IFES in Eastern Europe, Stacey Woods retired, and in 1978 Chua Wee Hian took over as General Secretary. It was, perhaps rightly, felt that IFES needed to correct a rather too overt orientation in its leadership towards the Western world. Years earlier, a student, then called Freddy Chua, had been at London Bible College. When he returned to Singapore it was to the IFES and in the intervening years Freddy, now known as Chua Wee Hian, had become Asia Regional Secretary. It was time for him to be appointed to the top job. How would Wee Hian, who moved the IFES office from Lausanne, Switzerland, to London, England, work with us Europeans coming, as he did, from a very different, Asian culture with a very different ethos?

He started by appointing Brede Kristensen as European Regional Secretary. Brede was a Dutch sociologist. IFES had never had a European Regional Secretary so this represented the beginning of a new structure in the fellowship. Many of the strong member movements in Northern Europe and Scandinavia were much older than the umbrella organisation, and could well have found it difficult to accept the need for a regional secretary, if only in fact to co-ordinate their outreach towards Eastern Europe. We the IFES staff also felt somewhat nervous. Here was our new boss who, together with his new boss, patently knew practically nothing about Eastern Europe. Yet we felt we needed his prayerful guidance, support and helpful perspective in the same way as Stacey had always given it.

Brede was certainly a useful link person. He strengthened contacts between the older stronger movements in Scandinavia, Holland and central Europe and used part-time visitors from these areas to encourage the people we knew in Southern and Eastern Europe. This was the time when graduate team and field partner schemes were being developed all over the globe. By 1980 ten or more co-workers or couples, typically university staff members or workers in other IFES movements, were travelling during their vacations. For example, Hans Jürgen Wennesland from Norway tried to encourage Polish schools work, Kees and Katonka Streefkerk from Holland visited Czechoslovakia, while Jonathan Neall was recruited from Operation Mobilisation to lead the East Europe team from his base in Heilbronn, Germany.

Once each year all these travellers tried to meet for a weekend. These weekends in a pretty Dutch village by a dyke were helpful for those starting to travel part-time, but I found them rather vague in focus. For several years, till conditions eased and by the end of the 1980's when staff from Eastern Europe could attend, they were the only specially convened annual staff meetings for twenty or so people. Each would be given five or ten minutes to present a picture of the work on their patch. Our debates seemed academic rather than real and the main benefit to be gained was usually from the address of a theological lecturer on a topical problem area.

It soon became clear that one visit each year was too little to be really effective. In addition to annual rucks in the theological carpet, the charismatic movement was, for example, gradually gripping all the denominations, there were also strong cultural parameters within each European country and without a good understanding of these deeply engrained ways of working, foreigners would inevitably continue to be just that, foreign. Then several people had to leave quite soon due to the demands of promotion at work or of small children arriving, while others found it too hard to squeeze several weeks for a useful trip into their busy academic schedules.

One very positive idea, however, was introduced, took root, and has blossomed down the years. It went under the curious acronym of EELAC—the East European Literature Advisory Committee. We on IFES staff felt like amateurs at Christian publishing until Jon Neall was recruited from Operation Mobilisation (OM) in 1979. Together with his OM colleague John Hymus who also had a passion for Christian literature they inspired all they met with the idea of translating thoughtful evangelical literature for each country. Our local collaborators, pastors and student leaders were consulted on title selection. Translations were then hammered out, often under exceptional difficulties. No one could be legally employed as a full time translator. Even when a willing person had produced a local version it could be lost to a police raid on their home. Many translations were never finished as parental or other pressures brought paralysing fears to those involved in this work. Despite all this a steady trickle of manuscripts began to arrive in the West, brought by courier. Specially adapted vehicles took the finished products back to Romania, Bulgaria, Czechoslovakia and other countries.

As the scale of activity expanded it became evident that an independent structure was necessary. So it was that the East European Literature Advisory Committee was registered as a Trust in England. Shortly afterwards Gerry Davey, who had 22 years' experience with OM in Christian literature ministry, was seconded half-time to develop this increasing work.

Throughout this period much thought and prayer went in to seeing how indigenous publishing could be structured in the East European countries as some of them, particularly Hungary and Poland, moved towards greater freedom in this respect. Could lessons learned here benefit future start-ups in the other countries? However the events of 1989 overtook us and 1990 found EELAC itself participating with others starting new publishing houses in Poland, Hungary, Czechoslovakia, Romania and Bulgaria. They were busy times as these publishing houses sprang to life like mushrooms after rain.

Since its inception EELAC has been vigorously supported by John Stott, the leaders of IFES, and OM and a large number of funding agencies. East European leaders selected titles of enduring value to build up the unity of the whole Christian community—books that challenged ideas without attacking personalities, that addressed root causes and stimulated a world vision.

Since the euphoric days of 1990, further publishing ventures have begun in St. Petersburg, Zagreb, Belgrade and Tirana. Several are now essentially self-supporting, charging realistic prices and learning to adapt to the market economies of their area. Between them they have at the time of writing published almost 800 titles. EELAC has an ongoing strong commitment to train and trust national colleagues and authors. Publishing houses all across Eastern Europe now openly employ people who worked clandestinely for years to bring helpful Christian books to people under regimes of varying hostility to anything Christian. This shows how fruit comes through careful preparation, even when the soil initially appears far from promising.

Meanwhile by 1979 despite our best endeavours to economise wherever possible and accepting enormous amounts of hospitality throughout Eastern Europe, we were living under increasing financial pressure. As a family of four, we were thankful for the produce from our garden which kept our living costs to a minimum.

I wonder now if I gave the job too much at this time. I was travelling more than ever in my efforts to prove how necessary I was to the operation. I felt I was being pushed almost to the limits of endurance. Or was I pushing myself? This had a very negative effect at home. I returned from a three month tour of south-eastern Europe, and Andrew, our younger son, did not recognise me! It was hard too for Anikó as I was playing a smaller and smaller part in home life. If the centre of an apple goes bad, you may not notice it for a while, but ultimately the whole apple is good for nothing. So too with family life—you can be very successful on the outside but not for long if it is going rotten at the core.

The signs were coming up that it would be good for all of us if we could change our working patterns, but in the event it proved to be a painful process. Repairing the links of home and family life, which I deeply cherish, was not easy and took quite some time. Fortunately these days the idea of a sabbatical—an extended time off for study, reflection and refreshment—is more widespread.

The work was exhilarating and rewarding but also a drain on my reserves. At the time I thought I was trying to do my best, but looking back I now believe it was more that I was trying to promote my career. In the course of this, I created my own difficulties. I thought IFES needed every ounce of energy I could give it but I was, in fact, ready to crawl away after ten tiring years. Perhaps I needed to become smaller. God doesn't need organisations to grow bigger and bigger. He is looking for smallness that generates faith and dependence on him. John the Baptist was chosen by God for a special strategic ministry. When his job was done he was very glad to depart saying "He must become more important while I become less important." (John 3:30).

I needed time to unwind from the constant travelling, from organising my journeys, from the report and letter writing. Working at home, my whole week was devoted to IFES for as many hours a day as I could manage. We spent Sundays with friends and at church, but found we had very little time even for existing friends let alone extending our social life. Looking back, it now appears as an undisguised blessing that I was able to leave the organisation at the end of 1979 and spend the time I needed with my family. At the time, however, I did not see it like that. I was told it was time for me to finish. However, I just felt I needed my job and the job needed me and I struggled to accept that changes had to occur.

Personal interests distort the clarity of one's self-perception, and this can have a bad effect on the individual, family, colleagues and the work. Far better to be at peace do one's best and leave the outcome with God. His purposes are always greater than either us or the horizons we presently see.

Anikó had been an involuntary unpaid employee, much like the legendary vicar's wife. As the boys grew and needed less of her attention, she also developed her own ministry away from the IFES Bible courses. She interpreted for Hungarians at the Royal Courts of Justice, the High Court in London, in the famous

Rubik's Cube case, and later at N.A.T.O. headquarters in Brussels when the Hungarian military were 'getting acquainted' with their Western top brass counterparts. She has interpreted at international Bible courses, particularly at many Schloss Mittersill and at church gatherings in various different European countries. Now, after many years of interpreting and translating for IFES, Anikó has a proper life of her own, an unpressured choice whether to be involved with my ministry or not. Her career has blossomed!

Students never remain students for long, so there is always the challenge of building a new team of student leaders in every place to share the gospel with their contemporaries. For staff, it is always tomorrow and the future which preoccupy the mind and the effort. "Keep on keeping on", a phrase which our first pastor in Newick, Gordon Diamond, used to apply regularly to our Christian lives is equally, if not more applicable to student work.

There was an IFES rule which said that field staff must retire at the age of 40, but there were so many exceptions to this rule that we felt the new generation might have somehow continued to use our skills to enhance their own. These experiences introduced an uncomfortable series of challenges into my life, which I was unprepared for. They caused me to reflect deeply on the whole episode. Re-ordering and changes are always needed in missions, as in other organisations. Even with much care and concern, it is notoriously difficult to create new organisations from old ones. Building new teams from old is an essential skill for any mission leader.

I was very fortunate to have my love of cooking to indulge and my garden to dig; you can get rid of a great deal of frustration and non-clinical depression while preparing a bed for runner beans. I also had a church fellowship which stepped in to support me magnificently, so that I could continue my ministry to Poland. Ten years earlier, I would never have dreamt that I would be able to do mission work and evangelistic camps, entirely independent of any formal mission society support. You are hardly old enough to retire at 40! I was, and still am, constantly being invited to minister among friends in Poland.

Chris Davies, who had grown to become our great family friend, was not so fortunate. We had worked with each other for more than ten years, and our views and values were similar on a whole host of subjects. Chris had been the most marvellous supporter, confidant and constructive critic. I relied on her for candid advice. She filled a crucial role in our group. She had been involved in the devising of our strategic aims, had a great vision for what students could achieve and how to get the best from people, wisely foresaw difficulties we might have faced, and was a tremendous team-builder. Chris had a background in English student work with UCCF which I lacked. I doubt whether I alone could have made half the mileage which we achieved together through her personal and professional contributions. For me, her loss as a colleague was terrible. Then we were all saddened by her serious depressive illness which began after she left the student work. She was in and out of hospital being treated for her depression for almost ten years, though she eventually died from a heart attack in the spring of 1992.

Do we know the future? In truth we are blind to what the future holds, but deeply blessed if we have come to know the Lord who holds our future in his hands. Can we chart our course through life? We may try to, but many apparently mature, well-adjusted and secure individuals may inwardly be struggling. The cracks show when hard times in the home or recession in the economy hits. How much better to follow in the way Jesus leads.

Is there life after IFES? Wrapped up in serving the Lord in the International Fellowship of Evangelical Students, I could have concluded that my commitment to lifelong Christian service would be equated with lifelong service in this fellowship. But there was a different road for me to follow. The God who made us and knows us better than we know ourselves is the one who can search and try our hearts ... and lead us afresh in his right ways.

There is always more to aim for. Life is never without a purpose. God has given all of us talents to develop and to use in his service. If we can go out in Christ's name to help others, in the way that we would have liked to be helped, they in turn can go on to help yet others whom we could never reach. The Kingdom of God is growing, and the gates of hell itself cannot prevail against it!

WILL YOU FOLLOW?

Would I do it if I had my time over again? Would I go to Poland, would I serve with IFES? Yes, you bet I would! But there are a few things I have learnt along the way which could help me and perhaps you, as you seek to know God's will for your life.

First I would be rather less romantic in my ideas about how God wants us to co-operate with him.

Do you know the romantic tradition of how the call of God comes to a person to work for him? We see the lonely individual meditating under the stars or, if it is Hudson Taylor, on the beach at Brighton and a voice, maybe from heaven, challenges him (it is usually a "him") to a new vocation. He takes it to be the voice of God, sets off on his travels and from then on works flat out for God through thick and thin.

There are various passages in the Bible which seem to reinforce that tradition: the call of Isaiah, a vision of God in the temple saying "Whom shall I send? And who will go for us?" And Isaiah says "Here am I, send me"; the call of the boy Samuel "Speak, Lord, for your servant is listening"; Paul on the road to Damascus; Peter, James and John in their fishing boats; but perhaps above all, the call of Abraham. You will remember that God created the heavens and the earth and then humans in his own image. His human creatures rebelled, Cain murdered Abel, the flood came and chaos, arrogance, sin and death reigned. In all that mess God called Abraham to set about the long process of reversing rebellion. He called him as one individual, alone, to the task of founding a family through whom the world would be put to rights again.

And in a sense this tradition gives a true picture. There are moments when each of us stands before his or her maker and business must be done on a strictly one-to-one basis, without fudging or sliding round the issue, without ducking or diving. But perhaps we enjoy this romantic tradition because it is remote from our own experience and we don't feel threatened or challenged by it. It is like watching a Superman film—we watch the hero in amazement. We get vicarious enjoyment and a feeling of satisfaction from achievements and then go home feeling better but without any personal engagement or commitment.

Throughout the Bible we see God wanting to work through people. He has limited himself in this way. We may not understand why but he sends out calls to obedience to his will. "I will be your God, and you will be my people". And there is a tension—as we see time and time again the people of Israel rebelling. They want a king, to be like all the other nations, when actually God himself wants to be their king. Later there are some good kings, and some bad ones. But the good ones who set their hearts to follow the Lord and obey his commandments are few, very few, in comparison to the many who lead Israel astray.

Let's look a bit closer at Abraham. He came from a good and respected family. He had a position in society, he was established, married, wealthy. He was the centre of a network of relationships, each one important and all quite complex. He was no starry eyed romantic idealist. When he stands out under the stars and talks with God it is as a real human being doing business with his Maker.

And his Maker tells him that he's got to be involved in a different business from now on. He's got to go with his wife and household, his flocks, and herds to a country he's never even visited before. He doesn't know the local language and he has to attempt a task he's never even thought of. We don't know how long it took for his call to crystallise but at some point he recognises it as the call of his creator to get going to do God's will.

How can you tell when it's the voice of God? That is a good question. I suspect it was often as hard for Abraham as it is for us. The fact that he is called the friend of God does not mean that it was any easier for him than it is for us. Sometimes we conclude that he misheard, misread the signals, got his wires crossed. But of the good news is that this did not seem to matter in the long run. The creator's voice was still to be heard—and you can tell it is him, because what he is talking about is precisely the restoration and renewal of his creation. "I made a lovely world, but up to now the human race has been lurching towards the cliff—arrogance, chaos, rebellion, despair. The world itself is out of control because its steward has abandoned his job. But Abraham, I am calling you to take the responsibility which Adam walked away from. I want you to begin that one unique family, through whom all the scattered families of the earth will be drawn together, reversing the tragedy of Babel. I want you to be my friend, so that the world can be healed." And Abraham, not the starry eyed idealist but the shrewd middle-eastern bargainer, takes his flocks, and herds and household, gets up and goes.

It's an ambiguous journey. Historians could classify it as just one more migration among the nomadic peoples of the area. Or sceptics could easily say that it was just a self-interested search for fresh fields and new pastures. They obeyed when they were called—more or less; they went where they were sent—more or less; and they did what they were told—at least some of the time. Read the story from Genesis 12 to 25 and you find an ambiguity and an uncertainty which looks a lot less like the romantic hero and a lot more like ordinary mortals. It may make a poorer Superman comic-strip, but it is a much more authentic start to the story of the people of God. Would we prefer it to be idealised—or are we are just glad that God could use someone who is not so distant from our own experience?

Because the call of God moves on. Abraham's family isn't founded so that humans can now be absolved from their responsibility to listen, choose, and act wisely in the world. It is founded in order to set people free to listen, choose and act wisely and by doing so to set others free and so in turn to set the world free to be God's world again. The promised land is to be a sign, a foretaste, of a whole new world order.

So God calls his people, Israel, in a series of beautiful prophetic voices that echo down through the Old Testament— to continue Abraham's task of being his people for the sake of the world. But Israel is as deeply divided or ambiguous as Abraham, if not more so. She is surrounded by many voices and drifts, this way and that, sometimes hoping she's following the voice of her God and sometimes hoping like Jonah, that she can manage to escape from it.

The story of Israel might be romanticised in children's Bibles but in the real Bible it certainly isn't. It's a messy story of muddled people who make false moves, take wrong turns but always, to their own surprise, find that some at least are brought back on track just when all seems to be hopeless. And as the night gets darker and darker, as Israel thinks she is so stuck in persecution and so squashed by foreign oppression, and when she is so sick and tired that many people are giving up on the whole thing, a strange thing happens again.

But again it is a bit ambiguous. There are some in Israel who were waiting and longing for God to act. Perhaps in many a Jewish girl's heart there was the dream that she might be the mother of the Messiah. And then Luke tells us how God sent the angel Gabriel and "Mary was greatly troubled and wondered what kind of greeting it might be." (Luke 1:29) And of course she said 'yes'. But we mustn't imagine that Mary was our typical heroine, grasping the promise of God and riding off with it through all the problems to emerge triumphant at the end. No, she had to sacrifice her dream before she came through to victory. She had to bear seeing her Son taking up with that shabby crowd down at the pub. If he'd lived today, she'd have seen him comforting and caring for AIDS victims. She had to watch as he was fawned over by the street girls—and he didn't even seem to mind. She had to bear watching when the occupying forces execute him as a failed Messiah. Here is the dark and hard side to the dramatic call of God.

When God called this woman to do his will, he called her to come and die—die to the hope she cherished, the hope she suckled, the hope born in her own womb and heart. Mary had been called to an ambiguous task—people would sneer at her when they saw her in the street, pregnant just a bit too soon. She saw her boy, her pride and joy, going off on a Messiahship quite unlike her idea of Messiahship when he was executed before her eyes. The call to do God's will is not to become the hero or heroine in God's new Superman story. It is to share and bear the pain of the world, so that the world can be healed.

And, if we want it, this is where we come in and it can become our story too. When Jesus arrived in Galilee, preaching the gospel of the Kingdom of God, the first thing he did was to issue a call which was remarkably like God's call to Abraham. You remember how that went: "Leave your country and your father's house, and go to the place I will show you, and I will make of you a great nation." Now it sounds like this: "Leave your business, your father's workplace, and come with me; and I will give you another job which will stretch you in new ways and draw out potential you never knew you had."

Again, we mustn't imagine that this call to serve came right out of the blue. There had been messianic rumblings and nationalist stirrings in Palestine for some time when Jesus arrived on the beach at Capernaum. We can be pretty sure that Peter, James and John were ready to go, and perhaps take along a couple of swords or flick knives with them. They were just the types who would want to, who would resent paying hard-earned money in taxes to the hated Roman occupiers, who would long to be able to bring up their own children in a free country, who might even—if they thought long enough about it—relish the idea of having the freedom and time to worship Israel's God and study the Bible. We can't say. But their motives, as later becomes clear from the rest of the Gospel story, were quite mixed. And yet they obeyed. They must have been the oddest rag-tag band of non-heroes you ever saw, an inept and bumbling platoon with a homegrown zeal, and a homespun philosophy. Hardly the sort to set the country on fire. But that was not the intention. *They* were the ones who were going to be set on fire. When God calls a man he calls him to come and burn—burn with a new love, a new desire, one that will take all the mixed and muddled ambitions and all that was God-given and purge out all that was obnoxious to God. This is the destiny of those who God calls—to be consumed by fire and to be on fire for him.

And it was this motley crew, this mixture of the obedient and the disobedient, this apology for a new people of God, who had their hopes shattered when Jesus went to Jerusalem to die instead of swooping down on it like Superman. When the crunch came they all ran away, apart from Peter, who stayed behind to deny his Lord. But soon after his resurrection they became the people through whom that old promise to Abraham began to be fulfilled as they went out into all the world to bring healing and reconciliation and life and love in the power and the fire of the Holy Spirit. God's call to serve is not designed to make us supermen and superwomen because that is not what the world needs. It needs men and women who are humble enough, and often that means humbled enough, to work from within, or from below, not to try to impose a solution on the world from a great height but to live within the world as it is, to live with the ambiguities and perplexities of their own sense of calling, to be in the place where they can listen for the voice of God and struggle to obey as best they can.

And the one place where Jesus said we could be sure of hearing the voice of God, his own voice, is in the cry of those in need—in physical, emotional, intellectual and spiritual need; the voice of the Spirit is groaning within the pains of the world. The voice of God does not call us to fix all the world's problems with a new programme of do-goodery but to be his feet, his lips, his hands—and remember what happened to those hands—his healing touch, his tears, yes, and his laughter too, in his world. We are to be ourselves with all our background, all the lives that our lives touch, all the ambiguities that we carry around with us but with all of these wonderfully transformed and taken up into the purposes of his love.

And we don't have to feel guilty if we aren't superpeople; rather we should feel guilty if we think we are. Nor should we mind if we don't experience a great romantic call when we are standing out under the stars—though it does happen from time to time. Some people do have such a call, others don't; it's all right either way. But what we must be doing, as individuals and also as members of wider communities and the worldwide Church, is listening to God. Within all the conflicting voices going on in our heads, on TV and around us, and in our ambitions and our secret longings, we must be listening for the genuine voice of our creator, our loving Father God, and ready to obey and do his will.

And if we listen carefully we may perhaps be able to hear the voice of God calling someone to follow Jesus for the very first time. Is he calling you to turn around and follow him rather than anything else? Or is he calling you to leave your country and work your heart out to bring healing in an inner city or go to a country far poorer than you can imagine? Or is he calling you to spend long hard years training for medical work or psychiatric work; or to look after handicapped children; or to enter the ambiguous, uncertain world of politics or to offer to serve in the ordained pastoral ministry?

And in and through all these calls may we hear God calling us to be wise and gentle in our relationships, to be sensitive and forgiving, creative and sustaining, to care for his world, his children, his Church. And the voice of God calls us all to rejoice, despite all our doubts and fears, in the fact that we have a God who has not left us to muddle through on our own but through blood and fire—his own blood, his own fire—has called us to follow him and do his work in recreating and healing his battered and beautiful world.

One day, when still a student at Leeds, as I was helping Raymond Turvey to hang wall-paper in his home, he told me how, as a young man, he had felt God calling him to Africa. He was ill then, so could not go. But later he still did not go. Yet God wonderfully blessed Raymond's ministry throughout his life as a pastor in England. I stood at the end of a meeting at Keswick to indicate my willingness to serve God anywhere he chose. For

10 marvellous years it happened to be on the staff of IFES. But that was not the end, either of my call or of the opportunities he has given to me to serve him. I used to be sad that so many missionaries went abroad to serve God but returned to their homes after less than a lifetime of service. Now I am glad that so many go to serve at least a few years—and then have a wider experience to contribute further to the restoration and renewal of his creation.

Is God calling you to share in doing his will? I hope he is. It is a wonderful privilege. May you be courageous like Abraham or Mary to follow him even if there are difficulties along the way. May you have a vision for what God wants you to do and then the strength to turn that vision into action. As David Livingstone, pioneer missionary and explorer in Africa said: "The fact which ought to stimulate us above all others is, not that we have contributed to the conversion of a few souls ... but that we are diffusing a knowledge of Christianity throughout the world ... We work for a glorious future which we are not destined to see ... We are only morning stars shining in the dark, but the glorious morn will break—the good time is coming yet."[23]

"This is the end of all the stories...
but only the beginning of the real story...
in which every chapter is better than the one before."

"The Last Battle" by C. S. Lewis, The Bodley Head, 1956.

References

"The Crown and the Fire" by N. T. Wright, SPCK, London, 1992

"The Growth of a Work of God" by C. Stacey Woods, Inter-Varsity Press, Downers Grove, 1978

"Some Ways of God" by C. Stacey Woods, Inter-Varsity Press, Downers Grove,1975

"Light and Life Renewal in Poland" by Grażyna Sikorska, Collins Fount Paperbacks, London 1989.

Notes

1 Growth of a Work of God, page 69

2 Stacey Woods in "Growth of a Work of God", page 54

3 Stacey Woods, "Growth of a Work of God", page 67

4 Ibid, page 59

5 Pastor Holmer spoke about having the Honeckers in their home. Local people knew they were there. They came and railed against them outside the Holmer`s home. Mrs Holmer went out to explain why they had taken the Honeckers in. And why? "We pray, »forgive us our sins as we forgive those who sin against us,« so we would be denying our faith if we had not been able to forgive them," explained Pastor Holmer. He continued, "Only once did we discuss our faith with the Honeckers. We told them that Marxism had made just one serious basic mistake. Marxism assumed that people were good. Change the environment, provide education and all will be well. Christianity did not make that mistake. Jesus starts with the human heart, which first needs to be changed."

6 Inter-Varsity Press, 1992

7 Inter-Varsity Press, 1978, page 37

8 "Growth of a Work of God" page 77

9 Ibid, page 94

10 "Growth of a Work of God" page 99

11 Ibid, page 37

12 "Growth of a Work of God" page 140

13 IFES Inc., while retaining some of the same board members, notably Yvonne Woods and John Bolten, has transformed itself into »Schloss Mittersill Christian Conferences and Study Centre«

14 "Getting Through Customs", Inter-Varsity Press, page 34

15 The Brethren Church was formed in 1918 by a union between some Lutheran and Reformed Christians with former Roman Catholics. By 1970 it claimed some 270,000 members. It has no connection with the (Plymouth) Brethren assemblies in the UK.

16 Grażyna Sikorska highlights the crucial help the "Light-Life" movement received from the West. ("Light and Life" pages 75-76) "Publication of Bibles and religious literature in Poland had been severely restricted due partly to the lack of funds but mainly due to the deliberate policy of the Polish State Authorities. It was not until 1965 that the Church was allowed to print the first few thousand Bibles since the end of the war. Not surprisingly the gift of over two million Bibles (in 1979) was received with enormous gratitude by the Polish Catholics. However, arguably the most touching example of Ecumenism at work came in the summer of 1981. Some 45,000 young people applied to attend Oasis retreats that summer—the last summer of the 'Official Solidarity'era. The country had already been plunged into economic chaos which was mostly engineered from the top but blamed on Solidarity. The shops were empty and people queued for hours to obtain basic food including bread. Solidarity was, needless to say, blamed for all shortages by the state controlled media; in stage-managed interviews seemingly ordinary citizens denounced the free trade union and called for tough government action. Food rationing was introduced and Oasis, treated as 'illegal camps' by the authorities, could not buy food. Some faint-hearted participants argued that under such circumstances the summer retreats should be cancelled.Father Franciszek would not hear of this. He immediately appealed for help to the West. Soon eleven trucks, each carrying twenty tons of food, arrived in Poland. They came from Austria, Norway, Denmark and France. In Norway, the twelve different branches of the country's Protestant Church cooperated together for the first time since the Reformation to run a very successful and united Oasis campaign. Thanks to the generosity of Western Christians the Oasis retreats were saved." (Grażyna Sikorska, "Light and Life Renewal in Poland" Collins Fount Paperbacks, 1989.)

17 John Stott was impressed by the turnout for Brethren Church services in Czechoslovakia. Writing in his diary about a visit to Dr Fazekas in Prešov he records »when I followed the pastor out of his house into the church building (a connecting door links the two), I was astonished to find it packed to the doors, with perhaps 300 seated and another 100 standing two or three deep in all the aisles...A choir of twenty men sang a Slovak hymn, a dozen little children sat on the bottom step of the platform, and after the service everybody stayed for a further half-hour of questions, so that we were in church for a good two hours.« For the evening service they travelled on to Bardejov, an hours drive to the north. »What was specially impressive about both services was the heterogeneity of the congregations. The ages ranged from very little children and babes-in-arms through teenagers and young people, adult couples and the middle aged, to dear old men and ladies, dressed in black, and bearing the stresses and sorrows of long life in their faces. They came from different cultural backgrounds too. There were farmers with tanned skin, and factory workers, alongside students and more educated professional people...After the service the pastor and I stood at the door. I'd just about learned to say »Do videnia« (»goodbye« in Slovak), and some of the men, the bearded and the beardless, felt free to give me the traditional East European greeting, a resounding kiss on both cheeks.« JRWS diary »Eastern

Europe, 9 April to 5 May 1980' quoted in »John Stott a Global Ministry« by Timothy Dudley-Smith, IVP, 2001.

18 On an earlier jaunt with me to Poland, in May, 1980, John Stott met memorably in Warsaw with Metropolitan Basil, head of the autocephalous Polish Orthodox Church, and wrote in his diary »I cannot describe him better than as a benevolent Father Christmas, nor a comparable occasion on which theology, whisky, coffee and ecumenical affairs were so harmoniously blended!« JRWS diary Eastern Europe, 9 April to 5 May 1980' quoted in »John Stott a Global Ministry« by Timothy Dudley-Smith, IVP, 2001, page 323.

19 Grażyna Sikorska, "Light and Life", page 138

20 Inter-Varsity Press, page 44

21 Ibid, page 45

22 Ibid, page 49

23 (Schapera (ed.) "Livingstone's African Journal", vol. 1, pp 57-58, entry for 22nd January, 1854, quoted by John Waters in "David Livingstone Trail Blazer", Inter-Varsity Press, 1996.

Index

Alphonsus, Niusia 79-81
Andjelić, Milenko 88
Austria 28, 54, 60-63, 81, 95, 103
André, Igor 75-78
Bailey, Fred 154
Balaton 98
Bán, Josef 76
Barciszewska, Ewa 128
Bednarczyk, Krzysztof 108, 109, 112, 123, 129, 130
Belgrade 88, 89
Berković, Daniel (Dado) 174, 177-179
Berlin 22, 35, 37, 38, 46, 168
Bernhardt, Dora 181
Białowieża 164, 165
Białystok 31
Bielice 81, 114-119, 122, 133, 137, 159-169
Bielsko-Biała 16, 88, 127
Bismarck, Otto von 12, 140
Bitterfeld 41, 42
Blachnicki, Franciszek 84, 85, 120, 121
Blair, David 114, 115
Błażowski, Tomek 115
Blocher, Henri 67
Bolten, Ernst F. 87
Bolten, John 61, 87
Boom, Corrie ten 75
Braşov 149, 150
Bratislava 18, 76, 78
Breslau (see also Wroclaw) 42
Brno 72
Brown, Harold O. Joe 24
Bucharest 94, 110, 133, 141, 142, 144-153
Budapest 15-18, 40, 96, 103, 105, 111, 129, 130, 172, 180, 182
Bulgaria 103, 120, 141, 155, 187
Bürki, Dr. Hans 25, 31, 57, 58, 65
Burt, David 118
Casa Moscia 57, 58, 60, 126, 128
Catherwood, Sir Fred 6, 67, 109, 179
Ceaucescu, Nicolai 133, 144
Cenian, Adam 168
Černý, Pavel 66
Charley, Julian 92
Chrapek, Witold 86-88
Chua Wee Hain 47, 57, 64, 102, 132, 185
Cieszyn 156
Cluj 143, 145, 146, 154
Cocar, Rodica 153
Cracow (Krakow) 30, 31, 35, 84-86, 94, 107-109, 112, 113, 116, 123-126, 129-131, 158, 162, 170, 172
Czechoslovakia 34, 36, 39, 44, 65, 66, 68, 71, 74-76, 80, 93, 104, 114, 119, 120, 126, 138, 155, 167, 186, 187
Dan, Pastor 145
Davies, Chris 91, 92, 105, 178-183, 190, 191
Davies, Ron 166, 168
DDR (see also East Germany) 36-48

Debrecen 92, 98, 99
Deva 146
Diamond, Gordon 23, 103, 190
Donji Miholac 94, 95
Dowsett, Dick 101, 163
Drava 95
Dresden 104
Dubček, Alexander 34, 44
East Germany 12, 34-48, 104, 138, 139
Engelbrektson, Ulla Bella 17, 18
Escobar, Samuel 67
Esztergom 16
Fajfr, Daniel 68
Fajfr, Dr. Vlado 69
Forster, Roger 175
Gdańsk 14, 30, 35, 40, 81, 118, 162, 163, 172
GDR (see East Germany)
Gdynia 28, 108
Giżycko 161
glasnost 12, 139
Glavnik, Pavlo 133
Gliwice 15, 107, 124-127, 156, 157, 159, 162, 169
Gorbachev, Mikhail 40, 139, 146
Graham, Billy 91
Graz 95
Grenfell, Frank 106
Grygar, Jiri 73
Grylicki, Miroslaw 14, 107, 125, 169
Haaften, Noor van 118
Hajnówka 164
Heath, Derek 117
Hegyeshalom 18
Heilbronn 186
Herjeczki, Kornél 180, 184
Hitler, Adolf 39, 135
Holekova, Marta 74
Holmer, Pastor Uwe 46-48
Honecker, Erich 39, 41, 46
Horn, Bob 32
Hradec Králové 73
Hunedoara 146
Hungary 14, 16, 25, 28, 32, 34, 36, 39, 40, 59, 91-93, 96, 98, 99, 103, 104, 111, 120, 126, 131, 138-141, 148, 155, 179-183, 187
Hymus, John 187
Iaşi 146, 151
IFES 11-13, 20-23, 25, 30, 32, 46, 49-52, 57-66, 81, 83, 88-94, 101-104, 106, 109, 111, 118-120, 125-128, 131, 132, 138, 139, 142, 145, 154, 155, 158, 176, 178, 179, 182, 185-187, 189-192, 199
IFES Inc. 60, 62
Jackman, Revd. David 134
Jagniątków 163
Jelenia Góra 163
Jonke, Mihael 83
Jonke, Nada and Gabriel 173, 176
Kaleta, Daniel 66, 68
Kálmán, Cseri 96
Kappelgaard, Arne and Ingeborg 91, 144-155
Karl-Marx-Stadt 46
Karlovac 174
Karpacz 163
Karwieńskie Błoto 163
Katowice 100, 115, 129, 156, 158
Kecskemét 97
Kielski, Prof. Andrzej 169, 170
Kircun, Alek 13, 165, 166
Kisoroszi 15, 16
Kitzbühel 61, 62
Kmethy, Anikó 15, 16 (Williams) 18, 23, 54, 65, 79, 88, 105, 109, 111, 129-131, 141, 167,
Kmethy, Győző 172
Knapp, Marilyn 77, 179
Komárno 18

Komárom 18
Kool, Anne-Marie 91
Kovács, Zoltán 180
Kowalczuk, Ruth 43
Kozince 158, 159
Kraków (see Cracow)
Kristensen, Brede 58, 144, 185
Kristinsson, Magnús 94
Król, Nina, Adam and Henio 155
Krynica 129
Kull, Erna 24, 65
Kutná Hora 66
Kuzmić, Peter 177
Laird, Dr. John 108, 112, 113
Lausanne 23-25, 65, 81, 101, 102, 185
Leeds 14, 17, 93, 94, 107, 108, 116, 125, 198
Leipzig 34, 41, 49
Lenzburg 25
Lewes 116
Lindfield 116, 117
Locarno 58, 60
Lokve 173-178
Lubicka, Beata 135
Lublin 39
Lucas, Dick 106-108, 134
Lum, Ada 56, 109, 110, 148, 151, 153, 168
Luther, Martin 10
Lwów 156
Maggiore, Lake 58, 60
Markby, Paul 116, 117, 134
Mickiewicz, Adam 124
Mikołów 162
Miksa, Robert 118
Minsk 7
Mittersill 54-56, 60-62, 64-67, 75-83, 86-89, 91, 92, 94, 103, 109, 110, 119, 125, 128, 142, 144, 145, 149, 155, 176-179, 182, 183, 190
Modzelewski, Żiutek 163, 168
Moscia 58, 60, 126, 128
Mostar 177-178
Muszkiet, Gustaw and Maria 118, 161
Nadachowski, Professor 123, 124, 129
Neall, Jonathan 186, 187
Newick 23, 167, 190
Niwiński, Janusz 118
Njeru, Newton 149, 150
Novi Sad 95
Nowa Huta 30, 123, 124
Odessa 141
Oleśin 163
Oradea 99, 143, 146
Orgovány 97
Osijek 177
Padilla, René 67
Paisley, Liz. 109
Pantz, Baron Hubert von 61
perestroika 12, 139
Pfeifle, Ernst 134
Plzeň 114
Poland 12-15, 17, 31, 32, 34, 35, 39, 42, 43, 51, 59, 79-81, 83-87, 91-93, 100, 101, 104, 106-108, 113-118, 120-128, 130, 131, 135-139, 141, 144, 155, 156, 159, 160, 164, 165, 167, 187, 190, 192
Potoček, Josef 73
Potsdam 35
Prague 34, 44, 66, 67, 72, 74, 111
prayer 24, 25, 47, 53, 61, 62, 65, 69, 72, 81, 83, 86, 92, 114, 130, 140, 150, 162, 176, 179, 186, 187
Prower, Józef 16, 17, 166
Pszczyna 125
Rasa 58
Remi, Georges 30
Richter, Dr. Klaus 44-46

Rijeka 173
Romania 12, 25-27, 91, 93, 99, 103, 104, 110, 112, 120, 133, 138, 139, 141-155, 177, 187
Salzburg 54, 60, 62, 63
Sarajevo 178
Schaeffer, Francis 12
Schloß Mittersill - see Mittersill
Securitate 26, 27, 144, 145, 147, 152
Senec 78
Sibiu 153
Skoczów 161
Sofia 103, 141
Sopron 28
Stasi 36-41, 101
Stott, John 78, 93-100, 111, 187
Stronie Śląskie 160
Studentenmission in Deutschland (SMD) 47
Stuttgart 94, 111
Sudár, Viktor 65
Szczytno 118
Szeged 96
Szentendre 15, 16
Tábor 66, 68, 73
Tamási 97
Ţepeş, Cristie 151
Thackray, George 17
Timişoara 110, 146, 147, 154
Tintin 30
Tito, Josip 94
Ţon, Iosef 146, 147
Tóth, József 15, 16
Transylvania 99, 143
Trhový Štěpánov 69
Trobisch, Walter and Ingrid 77
Turvey, Raymond and Mary 105, 107, 198
Tuzla 178
Tyndale, Tony 56
Tyniec 113
Ulbricht, Walter 39
Vác 16
Varna 141
Vavrišovo 76-78
Veselí 73
Vienna 17, 18, 29, 31, 40, 111, 154
Visegrád 16
Vistula (see also Wisła) 113
Volkmann, Dr. Bodo 119
Wajda, Andrzej 30
Wallis, John 101, 116
Warsaw 31, 44, 71, 108, 112, 113, 117, 124, 125, 129, 130, 163, 164, 171
Wieja, Henryk 166
Wieliczka 129
Wisła 113, 115, 158, 161, 163
Wojnar, Jan 17, 126-128, 166
Wojnar, Nelek 17, 166
Wojtyła, Karol (Pope John Paul II) 35, 84, 85, 131
Woods, Stacey 11, 12, 20-24, 33, 49, 51-53, 56, 57, 59, 60, 65, 102, 133, 138, 139, 184, 185
Woods, Yvonne 24, 65
Wrocław 42, 43, 79, 81, 116-119, 135, 161, 162, 165, 167
Würzburg 111
Yeltsin, Boris 140
Yugoslavia 11, 32, 82, 83, 92-96, 104, 138, 139, 177, 178
Zachanowicz, Ela 161
Zachanowicz, Niusia 114, 162
Zachanowicz, Stefan 163, 168
Zachanowicz, Witold 161-168
Zagreb 85, 93-95, 173, 174, 176, 177, 179, 188
Zell-am-See 62, 76
Zopf, Hartmut 44-47
Żegiestów 130

Nyomás: Royal Press Hungary Kft.
Felelős vezető: Lakatos Imre ügyvezető igazgató